D0445224

THINKING ABOUT THE NEXT WAR

ALFRED A. KNOPF

NEW YORK 1982

THINKING

ABOUT THE

NEXT WAR

BY

THOMAS

POWERS

The essays in this book were previously
published in *Commonweal*.

LIBRARY OF CONGRESS CATALOGING IN PUBLICATION DATA
Powers, Thomas.
Thinking about the next war.
1. Atomic warfare—Popular works.
2. World War III—Popular works. I. Title.
UF767.P68   1983   355'.0217   82-47930
ISBN 0-394-52831-X

For Clive

A wiser rule would be to make up your mind soberly what you want, peace or war, and then to get ready for what you want; for what we prepare for is what we shall get.

WILLIAM GRAHAM SUMNER, "War" (1903)

CONTENTS

INTRODUCTION

Like most writers, I imagine, I spend a lot of time in secondhand bookstores, and nothing else I find there is quite so dusty and unwanted as political books published between the wars. They must arrive as part of a lot. No sane book dealer would pay anything for most of them. Once they find their way onto the shelves, there they stay. For these books the peace of a bookstore is the peace of the grave.

Time has dealt harshly with them. The warnings all seem so obvious now, and yet at the same time curiously askew. Lots of writers got Hitler about right, but floundered helplessly when it came to explaining things or suggesting what ought to be done. Considered in hindsight, their books seem opaque and groping. Intense intellectual effort was required to see through the thick of events, and not many writers managed it. Nothing turned out quite as expected. Even personal accounts of the rise of Fascism, tragic as they sometimes are, have a faded, irrelevant air. To understand the events of those years, one has to know how they turned out. War settled everything with tremendous finality. Very little political writing from before the war retains anything but antiquarian interest. An afternoon's browse through that copious literature is a cautioning experience for any writer trying to understand the very similar situation in which we find ourselves now.

The essays collected in this volume have a central theme which is quickly stated: it is that we have not seen the last of big wars, and the next one will probably involve the use of nuclear weapons. Much the same—minus the nuclear weapons—might have been written between 1933 and 1939. If history is cyclic, we have come around again. Since 1945, the United States and the Soviet Union have been preparing to fight each other in a big war, and eventually they are going to do it. This is a bleak prospect, but I can't think of a way we might escape it—that is, a realistic way, one we might really adopt. We may want things to turn out differently, but wanting is not enough. Everything we have *done* is consistent with preparation for war. When the war comes, we shall fight it with the weapons at hand, and these prominently include nuclear weapons.

Does this mean that human history is shortly to come to an end? One naturally shrinks from thinking so, and yet it is increasingly clear that we have built a military instrument with the capacity to threaten not only ourselves, but the natural world itself. Many additional thousands of nuclear weapons will be added to American and Soviet stockpiles in the next few years. George Kistiakowsky, the chemist who designed the implosion lens used to detonate the first atomic explosions, felt from the beginning that we had invented the means of our ultimate destruction. The day after the successful Trinity test in July 1945, in the cafeteria back at Los Alamos, the *New York Times* reporter William Laurence asked him for his reaction to the test. Kistiakowsky replied, "I am sure that at the end of the world—in the last millisecond of the earth's existence—the last human will see what we saw."

In the spring of 1981 I asked him in an interview if he still felt the same way. He answered with great vehemence, bringing his hand down hard on the desk in front of him. "*Yes!*" he said.

We can never know the answer to this question. But even if Kistiakowsky is right in a general way, I doubt that the human race will end in quite the manner he described. If worse comes to worst, it seems more likely the last man will be some self-reliant type—an Appalachian subsistence farmer, a Macedonian shepherd, a !Kung from the Kalahari Desert—slowly succumbing to cancer of the pancreas. That last man might die hundreds of years after the last explosion, and he probably wouldn't know what was wrong with him, nor what had happened to everybody else.

Kistiakowsky's apocalyptic view of nuclear war is widely shared. Einstein himself once said he wasn't sure what weapons would be used in a Third World War, but that he was certain the Fourth would be fought with bows and arrows. The peace movement, which is now in a period of rapid expansion, for the most part argues we have got only one chance to avoid Armageddon, and that is now, before the shooting starts. The idea we might survive another nuclear war—Hiroshima and Nagasaki ended the first—is rejected with considerable heat. These critics insist we find ourselves faced with a choice of either/or: *either* we get rid of nuclear weapons and abolish war, *or* we destroy ourselves utterly. The logic of this position is strong, and it serves as a powerful organizing principle for a popular movement. The world is wedded to arms, and only the direst of threats might be expected to end this ancient partnership.

Nonetheless, I do not think that words alone—and it is of words that arguments are made—will be enough to end, or even much ameliorate, the military confrontation of the superpowers. If the appalling fact of Hiroshima has been swallowed by the world's military establishments, which continue to insist that preparation for war is the best way to avoid it, how can we expect mere entreaty to do better? The national security community in the United States—I assume its counterpart in Russia feels much the same way—is equally uncomfortable with talk of Armageddon or of "winning" a nuclear war, but it is confident it has got the situation well in hand, and can keep it that way so long as civilians do not dam the flow of money. In official circles, arms control agreements are generally viewed as a way of shaping, limiting, and directing the management of weaponry, not of doing away with it. I have never met anyone in the defense business who expected things to change in any basic way—*ever*. I take this as evidence that we shall go on as we are, perpetually ready for war, and that eventually we will slip or fall or stumble into war. That is how it has come in the past; why should we expect things to work out any differently now?

But further than that it is difficult to go. War is notoriously unpredictable. There is simply no telling in advance what people will do once a nuclear war begins. The next one could involve thousands of warheads, or only a few. It might be limited to Europe, just as the Europeans fear, or reach every corner of the globe. The great powers might not be directly involved at all. Other countries—Israel or India, for example—might use nuclear weapons against their neighbors before the United States and Russia do. Of one thing we can be sure, however: the use of nuclear weapons on human targets will have a tremendously sobering and braking effect on the survivors, just as Hiroshima and Nagasaki did. We had a second chance in 1945, but did not take it. We concluded that these weapons were too useful to give up; talk of international control was perfunctory and achieved nothing. The United States dreamed that it might retain a monopoly of the bomb for fifteen or twenty years. My own view is that we shall get still another chance to decide whether we want to go on trying to protect ourselves with nuclear weapons. The next time, reminded again of their destructiveness, and of the natural progression from preparation for war to war itself, we may decide differently.

The essays that follow were all published in *Commonweal* magazine, and were mostly written over the last two years. In the summer of 1980 I began doing research for a book on the history of nuclear weapons and delivery systems. It did not take long to grasp the basic outline of that history: more all the time since 1945, with the feeblest sort of progress in arms control and the improvement of U.S.-Soviet relations. Not only have the weapons become more numerous and powerful, but they increasingly threaten each other. Deterrence depends on the confidence that you can always strike back, and that confidence is eroding. Studying this situation in detail was a dismal experience, and I began writing these essays as a way of coming to terms with it, to figure out what I thought about these matters, and—I confess—to ease my mind. Most writing about nuclear war is limited to fact and theory; I wanted to say something about what it means in human terms.

The essays are printed here pretty much in their original form. The dates of their first appearance can be found in a bibliographical note at the end of the book. Such textual changes as have been made are mostly for the purpose of clarifying matters, forgotten now, which were in the news when I wrote. In one or two places I have expanded slightly a point in the original, but I have made no attempt at extensive revision.

One final word: I would like to express my thanks to the editors and staff of *Commonweal,* for which I have been writing a monthly column since 1975. If they grew weary of my preoccupation with nuclear weapons, especially during the year when I wrote about nothing else, they never let on. When they disagreed with my conclusions, they waited to say so—and then only in a spirit of thoughtful debate—until after the pieces had appeared. They have extended the sort of welcome a writer rarely gets, and I am grateful for their warmth and generosity. My particular thanks, then, to Jack Deedy, Jim O'Gara, Anne Robertson, Ray Schroth, Edward Skillin, and Peter Steinfels.

April 1982   THOMAS POWERS

THINKING ABOUT THE NEXT WAR

1. PEACE OF A SORT

Headline from the *New York Times* of November 23, 1975:

EXPERTS DOUBT VIEW
THAT ATOM BLAST
COULD END ALL LIFE

It's hard to keep some problems in focus. The poor, for example, are always with us, but it's hard always to think of them. The same goes for nuclear weapons. They have been with us for thirty years and a cause of—how shall we put it?—*continuing concern*, but most of the time we are thinking of other things. I know, roughly, what a bomb would do to Manhattan, where I live, but it's hard to look out the window and think that one day it will be a smoking plain. You see such things only in erratic flashes.

A dozen years ago, for example, I went up to Plattsburgh, N.Y., for an Air Force physical and spent the night in the Bachelor Officers' Quarters. My roommate was a young B-52 navigator who owned a 750 cc. Triumph motorcycle and a Corvette. Before he went to bed he did 50 push-ups and 100 sit-ups. After he finished we talked about his motorcycle, his car and his work. On an average day, he said, he took off from Plattsburgh around ten in the morning, flew down the East Coast to Atlanta, turned west to St. Louis, then north to Chicago and finally on back to Plattsburgh, arriving in plenty of time for dinner.

I asked if they carried nuclear weapons on board.

"Of course," he said. "That's the whole idea. Not to get caught on the ground."

I asked if he and his crew would have any hesitation about dropping their bomb, if it came to that.

"No," he said. "We have so many things to do, so many check lists to work through, that we'd be over the target before we knew it. Besides, that's what they pay us for."

I took him at his word.

Headline from the *Washington Post* of April 5, 1976:

ISRAELI A-BOMBS PUT AT 13

The major newspapers, newsmagazines and broadcast networks all have Pentagon reporters, and along with the stories about closing military bases they report from time to time on the ultimate question. They can write knowledgeably about first- and second-strike capabilities, "city busting," "throw-weights," deterrence, hard and soft missile sites, the difference between MIRVs and MARVs, and the like. I have no complaints about their seriousness or expertise, but sometimes I wish their language wasn't so flat, careful and judicious. Sometimes I wish they would describe the officials a bit, tell me something of their faces and voices when they argue for doubling the size of warheads. But it would be out of place, and it would absorb too much of their limited space, nudging out facts, and the news paragraph itself, short and dense, is unsuited to vivid writing. Besides, it's hard to maintain a sense of alarm.

I suppose that Leslie Gelb and Drew Middleton of the *Times* have their moments of sudden fear when they hear sirens at night, like everybody else. The art of the siren has made a lot of progress in recent years. They used to just wail, but now they warble, or let out foghorn blasts that make you all but start up out of your chair. Almost everyone will confess to the sudden half-fear—*is this it?* —when a siren catches them unprepared, but we would think it odd if Gelb and Middleton put that sort of thing into their grey columns of newsprint. Would their editors grow irritated if they insisted on appending a paragraph or two on radiation burn to every story? Would we? I suspect we would.

All the same I wish there were some way to make the danger seem real. It seemed real enough to me when I was ten and used to have air-raid alerts at the Siwanoy School in Pelham, just outside New York. We knew it was only practice, just in case, but I don't remember talking or laughing during the drills.

They led us out into the central corridor and sat us down on the linoleum floor, backs to the wall, away from the windows. They showed us how to bend over, heads between our knees, to protect our eyes from glare and shattering glass. That made it real for 20 minutes, but of course Gelb and Middleton can't go on repeating such stories forever. I, myself, have never written about this before, and I probably never will again.

Headline from the *New York Times* of February 1, 1976:

WORLD'S SPENDING
ON ARMS REPORTED
AT RECORD LEVELS

Study Places Annual Outlay
at $300 billion—Fastest Rise
in Developing Lands

U.S. and Soviet Account
for 60% of Expenditure
Gain Sharpest in Mideast

It is unusual for an arms story to make the front page.
The last one I remember was the ABM story, which
captured attention as much for its elements of political
melodrama as for the inherent significance of the proposed ABM program itself. The usual position for arms
stories is somewhere around page 13. They are almost
always one-day stories. Something is reported about the
B-1 bomber—a rise in cost, say, to $21 billion for a fleet of
244—and that is the last you hear about the B-1 for a while.

But if you were to clip the papers methodically for a
year or two you would notice, I think, how vast, inexora-
ble and immutable the world's arms programs are. In
every corner of the globe governments squeeze every
available penny of revenue or credit for arms. India, Iran
and Saudi Arabia are only three recent big spenders. The
passion for arms is universal. Every Palestinian kid in
Lebanon wants his own Kalashnikov assault rifle, just as
every national leader wants his own air force, and both
generally get what they want. This isn't entirely crazy. In
Deadwood, South Dakota, a hundred years ago it probably made a sort of sense to carry a gun, especially if you
wanted to carry money too. The difference here is that
the great powers carry guns of unprecedented caliber,
and that the world's well-being demands they *never* go
off. Never is a long time. It seems the more improbable
when you stop to consider that up until now the world's
great armies have *always* gone to war sooner or later. The
great fleet of Darius, the Roman legions, the Spanish
Armada and the Wehrmacht were all intended for war,

and that is what they were used for. Why should the present situation end any differently? Of course we all hope it will end differently, but is hope enough?

When you stop to think of these things clearly and logically, the situation looks bleak indeed. We have had peace of a sort for thirty years, but there was peace of an even better sort for forty-two years between the Franco-Prussian and First World Wars. We're not in the mood for war, perhaps, but we're certainly ready for it, and if we wait at the ready long enough, the mood may steal over us. I don't have the figures, but I would suspect that since 1950 every quarter has seen a rise in the number and size of nuclear weapons ready for war. Not only has the total megatonnage increased, but the means of delivery have steadily progressed as well. Missiles are more accurate and better protected. Their capacity for destruction is very great, although not quite as great as is sometimes supposed. My friend Tim Ferris, who knows a lot about these things, points out that even a really major nuclear war—what Herman Kahn used to call a "spasm war," in which everybody shot off everything—would not destroy all life. Human life, perhaps, but not all other sorts. The human episode on earth might be ended, but not the planet itself. That is what you would call faint comfort.

Take a minute right now and try to imagine all the people, all over the globe, who are ready—right now, at this very instant, whether you are reading these words at noon or midnight—to fire all the missiles. From South Dakota to Novosibirsk, and in all the oceans between, there are men on duty—at this very instant!—ready to push the buttons.

I know it's difficult to think of so many people in so many places, all at the same time. I find it easier to imagine the men on the aircraft carriers. They are far from being our first line of nuclear attack or defense, but they have their bombs too. In the summer of 1966 or 1967—I forget which—I spent a day on the U.S. Aircraft Carrier Saratoga in the Mediterranean, watching military exercises. Two things remain in my mind.

One was the Phantom jets taking off at night. The noise was simply incredible, even with ear plugs. The whole ship seemed to vibrate with the roar. The flame pouring from engine exhausts lit up the ocean more brightly than the moon. After a while the engines were backed down and the roar and the light disappeared, leaving a whisper and a fading red glow, no brighter than a cigarette across a football field, as the Phantoms shot off through the darkness toward their targets.

The other thing I remember was a tour the following morning of one of the hangar decks. We passed machine shops and storage rooms and aircraft in the huge between-decks space like a factory floor while our guide pointed out this and that, never at a loss for some statistic or fact. Then we approached an area where two Marines were carrying rifles on guard. There was no sign on the big door behind them and I asked why there were guards standing in front of it, thinking, A-ha! here's the brig.

Our guide said nothing. His mouth opened and he looked unhappy as he groped for some way to say he was not allowed to say.

So I thought, of course. The ship has a nuclear capability, and this is where they keep the bombs. I imagine they're still right there, in the same place on the same ship, if they haven't been replaced by better, bigger and newer models.

Headline from the *Washington Post* of February 9, 1976:

The "threat" was delivered in the summer of 1974 when Nixon told two members of the House, "At any moment I could go into the next room, push a button and 20 minutes later 60 million people would be dead." A second version of the quote has Nixon saying, "I can go into my office and pick up the telephone, and in 25 minutes 70 million people will be dead." The threat had to be "clarified" (by Sen. Alan Cranston, the source of the story) because it was not really a threat at all, but only a comment by the President intended to show how precarious the world was, and how important the pursuit of peace. In any event both versions of Nixon's comment strike me as hyperbolic, although the second is perhaps faintly more plausible than the first. I can't see how a President could trigger a spasm war with one button or one telephone call, out of the clear blue, just like that.

But that simply begs the point. There is no question that the President of the United States, or the Chairman of the Communist party of the Soviet Union, could, if he wished, and if he went about it with a clear head, trigger a political crisis which would precipitate a war. It might take a bit longer than 20 or 25 minutes, but the end result would be the same. This would be so awful that it is hard —perhaps even impossible—to imagine anyone doing it, but you might have said the same thing of the First and Second World Wars, too, with a little foresight, and yet they happened all the same. In 1890 the German military strategist Helmuth von Moltke (the elder) wrote:

If the war which has hung over our heads, like the sword of Damocles, for more than ten years past, ever breaks out, its duration and end cannot be foreseen. The greatest powers of Europe, armed as never before, will then stand face to face. No one power can be shattered in one or two campaigns so completely as to confess itself beaten, and conclude peace on hard terms. It may be Seven Years' War; it may be Thirty Years' War—woe to him who first sets fire to Europe. . . .

Von Moltke did not have all the details right, but the gravity of his foreboding was hardly unjustified. It took 24 years but war came in the end, and it was just as bad as he had feared.

No one wants war now, either, but they're ready for it, and they are getting readier. Nixon and Kissinger tried to do something about this, but we all know what happened to them. Carter tried as well. It is hard to get everybody to agree on the same policy at the same time. When Kissinger was working on détente, Anthony Lewis of the *Times* was writing about Valery Panov, the dancer, who couldn't get a visa to leave Russia. We got Panov, eventually, but where is détente?

In the summer I go to Vermont, where my family has a farm. There is an abandoned pasture on a mountaintop across the valley, where the view and the blackberries are both magnificent. I take the children sometimes and after we are tired of picking—which for them comes very quickly—we lie on the grass and look up at the sky. Once in a while, way up there, I see a white vapor trail. It is so high up there is no sound. All my life I have seen those vapor trails, like a scalpel cut across the blue, but until I went to Plattsburgh I never knew where the planes were coming from, or where they were going. Now I know, and I think: One day all the planes will go up at once, and no one will call them back.

But then the children grow restless, and it's time to take them home, and I forget.

2. THE NEXT WAR

From John Hersey's *Hiroshima:*

> Mr. Taminoto . . . was the only person making his way
> into the city; he met hundreds and hundreds who were
> fleeing, and every one of them seemed to be hurt in some
> way. The eyebrows of some were burned off and skin
> hung from their faces and hands. Others, because of pain,
> held their arms up as if carrying something in both hands.
> Some were vomiting as they walked. Many were naked or
> in shreds of clothing. . . .

We know all that:

100,000 dead in Hiroshima, Nagasaki, Dresden, Hamburg. The horrors of war have not been kept a secret.
We've read about napalm, cluster bombs, free-fire zones
in Vietnam, starvation in Biafra. Photographs have
helped us to see. We're well-informed. Everyone agrees
war is a terrible thing; no one has been able to do anything
about it.

One thinks of war the way one thinks of his own
mortality: in flashes of great clarity—suddenly, vividly,
intensely—and not for long. It comes and goes. A picture,
the odd sentence buried in a news story, a piece of film
on television—like a pain in the chest, a lump under an

arm—will make us see that this is real, such things happen, they might happen to us. We live with war the way we live with disease and old age. People really get cancer. The nursing homes are filled. Wars really happen. We know all that.

The fear of war is not of much use. We've been afraid of war for nearly 35 years, since the end of the last big one. In the meantime we've been in two smaller wars. We've spent a trillion dollars for old wars, present wars, potential wars, other people's wars, and the next war, and we've done it with a good working knowledge of what war involves. It is not only fear we've experienced, but the awful sense of futility and resignation, the anguish of knowing what waits in the wings, the shame of not caring, pity, guilty forgetfulness. None of it matters, none of it works.

Before long, if the papers are to be believed, the United States and Russia will sign a second SALT treaty limiting —perhaps directing would be a more accurate word—the development of nuclear arms.* The Senate must then decide whether or not to ratify the treaty. The argument is sure to be an emotional one, but whatever the outcome, nothing fundamental will change. Both sides will retain a capacity for destruction on a scale beyond the limits of human imagination, however well-informed. Some of us will allow ourselves to pretend for a time that SALT matters because it is a step, a symbol of commitment, a gesture of hope and possibility. But nothing will change.

---

*The treaty referred to here was signed in Vienna in June 1979, but withdrawn from the Senate the following January, after the Russian invasion of Afghanistan.

From a report of the bombing of Nagasaki by William L. Laurence in the *New York Times,* September 9, 1945:

> I watched the assembly of this man-made meteor . . . and was among the small group of scientists and Army and Navy representatives privileged to be present at the ritual of its loading in the Superfort. . . . It is a thing of beauty to behold, this "gadget." Into its design went millions of man-hours of what is without doubt the most concentrated intellectual effort in history. Never before had so much brain power been focused on a single problem.

This struggle—if such a mismatched conflict can be awarded the dignity of the word "struggle"—has already been lost. The development of nuclear weapons has been a headlong torrent. Their destiny is to be used in war. When the logic of events is a terrible one it becomes clear only in retrospect, after the facts have already crushed hope. Imagine for a moment that a nuclear war has taken place. Don't concern yourself overmuch with the details of when, or where, or between whom. There are plenty of possibilities. You have survived, as so many survived Hiroshima and Nagasaki. You have time to reflect, whatever may be still waiting in the wings. Ask yourself: did anything, in the years after 1945, ever suggest a different outcome?

One would not have to spend years in a library to find the answer. It is plainly before us now. The capacity for destruction has been growing at an exponential rate for 35 years, without any change in the autonomy of nations to prepare for, threaten, or wage war. The confrontation of the United States and the Soviet Union has been profound, complex, broad in scope, volatile, intermittently critical, and ceaseless, just like the other great confrontations of history between Athens and Sparta, Rome and

Carthage, England and France, Germany and the rest of Europe.

Once great powers are set upon a collision course it is difficult to deflect them. Diplomacy and prudence may ease them by one potential occasion for war after another, but eventually prudence fails, the diplomats cannot find words to disguise the unacceptable, and war follows. This pattern is the great commonplace of history. There is a kind of fatality about it.

Was the pattern of confrontation and crisis before the First World War fundamentally different from the pattern which preceded the Second? Have we any reason but hope for saying it is different now? Have the two SALT agreements done more to limit missiles than earlier efforts to limit navies? Has the United Nations been appreciably more effective in deflecting war than the League of Nations? It has taken 35 years for us to agree to build only enough nuclear weapons to wreck the world. Time is not making Hiroshima fresher in memory. The rise of China has only muddied the waters. Looking forward we imagine there is still a way out. Looking backward we see there was none.

But you can't write the history until it's happened. The details are necessarily obscure. Only the pattern is clear. Something alters the atmosphere, probably the fact or prospect of a strategic defeat. Perhaps the Eurocommunists come to power in Italy and France, and turn out to be Stalinist after all. Perhaps the King of Saudi Arabia joins the Shah in exile, and their successors invite Moscow to buy oil at five dollars the barrel. Perhaps the Chinese change their minds and drive for Hanoi, or the Russians determine on a pre-emptive strike against Lop Nor, or the Poles and Czechs find a way to secede from the Warsaw Pact, or Moscow and Peking patch things up and sign a 50-year Anti-Imperialist Friendship Treaty. These are the nightmares of the world's statesmen. Any one of them would leave some great power feeling desperate and vulnerable, a prescription for clouded judgment. Such things have happened often. War follows. No mystery will attach to it, in retrospect.

From Hersey's *Hiroshima:*

> Father Kleinsorge went to see her several times. On his first visit, he kept the conversation general, formal, and yet vaguely sympathetic, and did not mention religion. Miss Sasaki herself brought it up the second time he dropped in on her. . . . She asked bluntly, "If your God is so good and kind, how can he let people suffer like this?" She made a gesture which took in her shrunken leg, the other patients in her room, and Hiroshima as a whole.
>
> "My child," Father Kleinsorge said, "man is not now in the condition God intended. He has fallen from grace through sin." And he went on to explain all the reasons for everything.

Let me concede that none of the experts agree. They are almost giddily optimistic. In public, of course, they speak in solemn tones of the dangers—of proliferation, of Russian military supremacy, of a runaway arms race, of accidental war, or war between marginal nuclear powers, even of all-out spasm war. But in private they explain why they're not worried: war between the great powers just doesn't "make sense." There is nothing to be gained commensurate with the loss. Every nuclear power soon discovers just how destructive these devices are, and grows sober in response. The devastation would be "unthinkable." You'd have to be "crazy" to attack a nuclear power with nuclear weapons. "Common sense" precludes their use.

This attitude is nearly universal in professional circles. It is held by defense intellectuals, intelligence analysts, military strategists, high civilian officials of the Defense Department, Rand Institute consultants, generals, arms negotiators, and just about everybody else in the national security community. There are two related reasons for its prevalence. First, pessimism cannot serve as the basis of a career. If it doesn't happen in two years—war, the extinction of whales, devaluation, the end of the oil, whatever—your judgment has been discredited. Bertrand Russell and C. P. Snow were ridiculed for predicting nuclear war "in the next ten years" back in the mid-1960s. All the warnings will have been amply justified if it takes place in the next *hundred* years, but no official can go on predicting disaster for longer than the life of one Congress without losing the ear of his colleagues.

The second reason is even more briefly stated: the experts are as frightened of nuclear war as anyone else. They don't want one, and allow themselves to be privately hopeful, much in the manner of oncologists determined not to worry about getting cancer.

But that doesn't explain why they base their private optimism on common sense. Common sense is hardly what we depend on for the solution of most serious problems—poverty, the drowning of dolphins in tuna nets, an unfavorable balance of payments, segregated schools, crime, lead from car exhaust, famine in the Sahel, fraudulent advertising, toxic food additives, high medical costs, religious prejudice, the dumping of Japanese steel, oil dependence. These all justify, and in varying degree get, serious attention and practical efforts toward reform or amelioration. A nuclear war would make such problems look immaterial. Why do the men who know most about nuclear weapons depend on something so demonstrably feeble as common sense to prevent their use?

Because there is nothing else.

From an interview with Zbigniew Brzezinski in the *New York Times* of December 21, 1978:

> SALT fits into our broader effort to enhance national security, an effort which we pursue not only through improving our own forces, but also, where appropriate, through arms control. . . . In this context, I can assure you that we will never constrain our ability to meet our national security needs. A satisfactory SALT agreement will allow us to maintain the effectiveness of the United States strategic arsenal as a deterrent against nuclear war, based on a credible retaliatory capability in the event war should break out.

If peace is the universal aspiration of man, war is his natural condition. An academic study of international wars between 1816 and 1965, published in 1971 by J. David Singer of the University of Michigan, concluded that 93 wars had taken place during this 150-year period, that 29 million men had died in battle (civilians were not included), that there were 6.2 wars in the "average" decade with dramatic high points every 20 years or so, that Europe was the most war-prone part of the world (followed by the Middle East), and that on the average a war began every three years. The technology of war obviously improved by leaps and bounds during the period, while efforts to control, limit, prevent, or end wars made no appreciable progress whatever. It does not take a statistician to extrapolate the future from a pattern of such pronounced consistency.

Presently the world is armed as never before. At least seven nations—Russia, the United States, France, Britain, China, India, and Israel—have nuclear weapons and sophisticated means for their delivery. It is possible, but unlikely, that any country would fire off all it's got, even if backed into a corner, and it is still less likely that all the nuclear powers would fire off all they've got. This means that a nuclear war would not end the danger of nuclear war. Very possibly the opposite would be the case, once national leaders got over their initial surprise at not having completely destroyed the world.

Nevertheless, the most favorable moment for true arms control is immediately after the shooting stops, while the odor of the consequences is still in the air. The last such opportunity came to nothing, as the habit of militarism reduced the horror to fine words. I do not think it is a counsel of despair to suggest that the time to prepare for the next favorable moment is now.

3. ON DISBELIEF

I have never seen a nuclear warhead. But in the spring of
1981 I visited the Atomic Museum at Kirtland Air Force
Base on the edge of Albuquerque, New Mexico, and saw
a great many bomb casings. When you look at them your
eye says *bomb!* but your mind says they are just hollow
shells. The bomb guts are missing. Still, you get the idea.
Some match your idea of what a bomb ought to look like—
Fat Man, for example, the 10,000-pound bulbous monster
which destroyed Nagasaki. The one in the Kirtland
Atomic Museum is painted olive drab. The one at the
Bradbury museum at Los Alamos is painted white. Both
are grossly fat and thoroughly lethal in aspect.

But scariest of all is the Mark 17 bomb casing. According to the sign, this was the first hydrogen or fusion or
thermonuclear bomb which could actually be dropped
from an aircraft, but it's hard to credit. It's hard to imagine anything could get it off the ground, short of a der-
rick. It is 21 feet long and 5 in diameter and it weighs 24
tons. But the numbers don't suggest the impression. The
designer of the Atomic Museum had talent and a flair for
the dramatic. The displays are in a great cavernlike hall,
dramatically lit from below, and the Mark 17 looms up in
the gloom like a . . . well, quite a lot like the great blue
whale which hangs from the ceiling in the American

Museum of Natural History. The thing is *so* huge, the casing is *so* massive you simply can't believe it could get off the ground. But like all the others it's hollow. It's not really a bomb at all, just a suggestion of the bomb, nothing more than a teaching aid.

At Vandenberg Air Force Base a year ago I saw a Mark 12-A re-entry vehicle, a black cone-shaped object, perhaps three feet high, with a carbon-carbon skin and a polished nose cone of specially heat-resistant alloys which erode away in the terrible heat and wind of re-entry at ten thousand miles an hour. It was sitting in a classroom where Air Force officers take an introductory course in ballistic missiles. One of the instructors began to rattle off statistics and then stopped abruptly. "Sir," he said, "what is your clearance?" I said I was a journalist and didn't have any sort of clearance. That was the end of the lecture. But I marveled at the RV all the same. It was so small, light and sleek. Is there any limit to human genius? Somehow the guts of the Mark 17 leviathan had been refined and reduced and squeezed into this neat package a couple of men might cart off in a wheelbarrow.

So I've never really seen a bomb—just drawings, photographs, and the outer skins of bombs. Most people haven't seen the skins. For us the bomb is a purely mental thing, an abstract concept, a kind of pocket of anxiety in the mind. I *know* the New York City subway system is going through hard times, because I ride it every day. I *know* the price of gasoline is up. The sting in my eyes tells me Los Angeles has an air pollution problem. No one has to tell me that blacks and Puerto Ricans live in a different world, because I brush their shoulders on the city's streets. Things physically present announce themselves unmistakably, but the bomb is like the knowledge of death. It comes and goes, a kind of mood. A story in the paper, or a siren late at night, can bring it heaving up out of the unconscious part of the mind. But then it sinks back, like other things we know but can't bear to think about.

In the last two years I've talked to a lot of military people about nuclear weapons, strategic policy, what the Russians are up to, and the like. For the most part, they have been an impressive group of men—sober, intelligent, knowledgeable, and orderly in their habits of mind. They did not seem at all warlike. Nothing they said suggests that the defense of the United States is in careless or reckless hands. The motto of the Strategic Air Command, which has authority over bombers and land-based intercontinental ballistic missiles, is "Peace Is Our Profession." As I remember, it's carved on the lintel over the main entrance to SAC headquarters at Offut Air Force Base near Omaha. This is the sort of thing to invite a bitter smile, everything considered, but so far as I could tell, SAC people take it seriously. I asked a colonel at Offut if he thought the ICBMs would ever be launched, and he said no—they *all* say no—and added, "If that happened, we would have failed in our job." It's tempting to poke ironic fun at such earnest remarks, but it wouldn't be fair. The officer really meant it. His job was preventing wars, not winning them.

The military men involved in nuclear weapons policy —and their civilian colleagues, too, for that matter—don't believe it's ever going to happen. For them, I suspect, no belief is deeper and stronger. Their assurances on this point have none of the tinny quality of budget officials, say, telling you the federal deficit will disappear in 1984, when they know full well this barely qualifies as even an honest hope.

When you think about it, the equanimity of military

people makes perfect sense. They know the United States and the Soviet Union have got 15,000 strategic nuclear weapons between them. They've been trying to figure out a way to fight a genuinely limited nuclear war for thirty years, and haven't come up with anything convincing yet. They know the Pentagon periodically tries to plan for the post-attack world but always throws up its hands in despair because there is simply no way of projecting how bad it would be. The destruction would be too general. The normal means of recovery and reconstruction would be threatened in too many ways to calculate.

Take transportation. Airfields, ports, railway marshaling yards, and major highway intersections would be destroyed. Aircraft, ships, rolling stock and large numbers of busses, trucks, and cars would be destroyed. Many of the factories which might build more would be destroyed. If factories remained, the workers might be dead or too sick to work. The breakdown in transportation would make it hard to feed or care for them. Power lines would be out. Most petroleum refineries would have been destroyed, fuel would be in short supply, and the little remaining would be hard to distribute. And so on and so forth. How can you predict how long it would take to get things moving again when so many factors are involved, which overlap in so many ways? The answer is, you can't. The government goes on churning out civil defense and reconstruction plans, but the Pentagon has never made a serious official guess how well they would work—or even if they would work at all—because the computers can't factor in all the variables.

This is the sort of thing military men know, generally in great detail, and none of it is encouraging where the subject of nuclear war is concerned. On top of that, they *know* we shall never get rid of nuclear weapons. Arms agreements *may*—even that is in doubt—limit their number and type, but disarmament is not on the horizon. It is not *over* the horizon. When you put these two things together—knowledge of what nuclear weapons can do, and a conviction we shall always have them—you can see why military men tell themselves, and everybody else, the bombs will never be used. They are flesh and blood, after all. Their wives and children all live in target areas. They can't *bear* to think anything else.

It's difficult to remember how I thought about things a couple of years ago, when I first started to read seriously about nuclear weapons. A lot of things came as a shock then which seem familiar now. I made lots of errors in writing about the subject. Once, for example, I wrote that the bomb dropped on Nagasaki was the last one in the American inventory. In late August, 1945, I thought, there were no bombs in the world at all. But later the man who assembled the core for the fourth bomb told me I was wrong.

After two or three months of reading I went through a period of intense sadness. At first I didn't know what it was. I thought the source might be worry about my father, who is 89, or a friend whose marriage was breaking up, or chronic financial anxiety, or something else of the kind. Then I told myself I was an idiot. Of *course* I was sad. I had finally schooled myself in the numbers and knew for the first time that we *really had* built weapons enough to break the back of our civilization. I'd gotten the details straight about radiation sickness, theories of war-fighting which all imply any nuclear war will go the limit, the steady march of technical improvement in weapons design which makes military people so jumpy, and so on and so forth. I had read or been told *nothing* which suggested we were going to learn to get along without these weapons. It was quite clear, in fact, that we were going to go on pointing them at enemies until we used them or the world came to an end. Since the news on the geological front is all good, and the planet can expect to survive another couple of billion years, that meant, as a practical matter, we would go on as we were until we used them. In short, it seemed to me as clear as night follows day that it is going to happen.

But everybody I talked to took the contrary view. Everybody, that is, professionally involved in defense matters. Ordinary citizens often entertain foreboding of the darkest sort. In a quite matter-of-fact way they will say, "What else were they built for?" Defense community people *never* say that. What they say is, "It doesn't make sense. There is nothing to be gained. No rational man would ever use nuclear weapons. They can serve no useful purpose in war."

That, of course, is true enough. But does that mean they won't be used? You might have said all those things about the great armies of Europe in 1914. Indeed, people did say them. Reasons for not using nuclear weapons are also reasons for not having them. Citing the litany of their horrors is an argument against their possession or use, not an argument we won't use them—given we have them. Such arguments are really an expression of hope, and we depend on hope because there is nothing else. I have heard dozens of defense people explain why nuclear weapons will never be used. I have *never* heard a note of fear or despair. Their confidence is sunny and unshakable. If we just stick to our guns and make sure we've got a weapon for every weapon they've got, then there's nothing to worry about. There is a soothing quality to these reassurances, as if we were being told that airplanes really do work, and it's safe to fly.

But now comes the curious thing. After a year or two of seeing things in this light, for the first time I feel the tug the other way. I find myself wondering if perhaps the military men aren't right after all. They say it would be crazy, and are absolutely right. We worry about so many things that fail to come to pass. Two hundred years ago Malthus was worrying that the world's population had already stretched the planet's resources to the groaning limit. Maybe fear of nuclear weapons is enough to keep everyone sober and cautious. Maybe the only danger is falling behind, just as the Pentagon says. Maybe all those people in Washington are right, and I'm wrong. I devoutly hope they are right. Maybe it just won't happen.

This is a mood I'm describing, not really an argument. I don't believe it for a minute.

The problem is disbelief. An argument is the ephemeral stuff of the mind. It has no solidity. It surrenders to the world, over time, and the world tells us tomorrow will be much like today. It is a considerable undertaking to go out and see the Air Force bases and atomic laboratories and missile-launching centers. But even there the note of the lethal is missing. The bomb casings are all hollow. The missiles are all mock-ups used as teaching aids. The military men work eight to four and go home to their families. Nobody shows any sign of fear. Everything suggests tomorrow will be much like today.

We know we are mortal but we don't feel mortal and we live, generally, as if there were plenty of time for everything. The moments of recognition are few and they fade. We know that nothing lasts, nations die, the continents move, atmosphere whirls off into space, suns burn out—but not here, now, to us. These things we can't believe. It is the same with the missiles in their silos. We know what they will do. Most people don't even have to be told. They *know*. But knowing and believing are very different things. The world has its disconcerting way of going on from day to day, just as if nothing were ever to change. Belief is frail and fades away.

The people in the defense community have all had their ghastly moments, from the president on down to the missile-launch control officers reading paperback novels forty feet beneath the Great Plains. Every last one of them, I am convinced, has looked it in the eye at one time or another. Even Nikita Khrushchev had his dark moment. He once told the Egyptian journalist, Mohammed Heikal, "When I was appointed First Secretary of the Central Committee and learned all the facts about nuclear power I couldn't sleep for several days. Then I became convinced that we could never possibly use these weapons, and when I realized that I was able to sleep again." Thus we all go on, sustained by disbelief.

4. WAR BY COMPUTER

If you'll think about it for a minute, you'll see why it makes sense to fight a nuclear war by computer. Since the United States and the Soviet Union can both deliver thousands of warheads, and since launch-to-target time can vary from several hours down to three or four minutes, and since the results of the first half of the war logically ought to determine strategy in the second half, the job is simply too big and complicated for anything like a traditional commander. The fact is it has all been worked out on paper and turned into software called the Single Integrated Operating Plan, or SIOP for short. What the plan is we don't know, but it has been programmed into a computer deep underground at Cheyenne Mountain in Wyoming. In the event of a major attack—that is, in the event various sensing systems pick up the launch of many missiles and feed the information to SAC's computer—SIOP will go into effect.

This makes sense, but it also raises questions about computer reliability. Programmers make mistakes and computers do too, sometimes of an eerie, otherworldly kind. Not long ago a computer made a mistake at the North American Air Defense Command (NORAD) headquarters in Colorado Springs, Colorado. The cause of the mistake is unclear, because the Pentagon isn't telling. It was described as a "mechanical error," which suggests that somebody pushed button "A" instead of button "B." The effect, at any rate, was to feed information from a routine war-game tape into NORAD's computer in such a way that the computer thought a Russian submarine in the North Pacific had launched a handful of missiles toward the United States. Of course the computer sounded the alert, jet interceptors scrambled in the United States and Canada, and the men deep underground at Minuteman control panels had an anxious few minutes wondering if the moment had arrived to turn the brass key. But that's as far as it went; there are many safeguards against this and other possible errors and within six minutes, according to the Pentagon, the NORAD computer was pacified.

The fear of an accidental war runs deep, with good reason. Reaction time is so short there is little margin for error. The United States has so far resisted a policy of launch on warning, despite its obvious military advantages, precisely because it increases the danger of accidents, as well as the danger of miscalculation. "Mechanical error" is far from being the only possible sort. What if a sizable chunk of nickel-iron from deep space should land on downtown Washington some hot August night? An eon ago a meteorite perhaps fifty feet in diameter left a crater the best part of a mile wide in Arizona, and something devastated a large corner of Siberia back in 1907. An ordinary pair of binoculars will show you what meteorites have done to the moon. Would a similar catastrophe on earth trigger a spastic nuclear reaction?

The answer is no. The Pentagon has thought about this a good deal—one hopes the Russians have, too—and there is very little chance of anything except a nuclear attack being perceived and responded to as a nuclear attack. But the public is hard to reassure on this point, and it is quick to fear that things might somehow slip out of control.

A vivid image sticks with me from a movie of the early 1960s called *Failsafe*. The word "failsafe" refers to the military command and control procedures which are intended to prevent a nuclear war from starting by accident. In the film a nuclear alert was triggered by something trivial and unexpected—a flight of geese, weird atmospheric effects over the Arctic, something of the sort —and a flight of B-52s carrying bombs was routinely started on its way to Russia. As soon as the initial error was identified, an order went out telling the B-52s to head for home, which they all did, with one exception. As President Kennedy said during the Cuban missile crisis, "There's always some SOB who doesn't get the message."

The crew of the lone B-52, convinced that at last push had come to shove, was determined to do its duty. An ordinary crew of American boys, half cowboy and half bank clerk, determined to do and die because there would be nothing to come home to anyway. A squadron of U.S. fighter planes was sent after the B-52 over the Arctic, but they were too late, and one by one they ran out of fuel and nosed down in strange silence toward the pack ice. That's the image which sticks with me. It was an awful cinematic moment, when you realized nothing could be done. The Air Force protested the movie on the grounds things didn't work that way, the B-52s required a positive go order and would automatically turn back without it, but that didn't detract one whit from *Failsafe*'s impact.

A similar catastrophic accident was at the heart of Stanley Kubrick's *Dr. Strangelove*. There a loony Air Force general named Jack D. Ripper, convinced the Russians were poisoning the American water supply, ordered the planes aloft and Slim Pickens rode the fatal bomb out the bomb-bay door as if it were a Brahma bull. Of course Kubrick was pushing things farther than they are ever likely to go, but a residual popular distrust of the political sophistication of generals lingers all the same. Those rigid men with their crewcuts and knifeslash mouths and narrow-eyed suspicion of the Russkies seem frail vessels for the awful authority of the bomb. The Pentagon may protest all it likes that no general or admiral has any such authority, but the truth is they have something close to it, and respected civilian strategists have worried that some brigade commander in Germany, or some naval captain in a Trident submarine off Vladivostok, might take it into his mind to stand up straight and let 'em have it, because he thought the president was caving in. Sentiments of that sort, at any rate, are not hard to find, and technical considerations necessarily reserve a certain autonomy for the men in control of submarine-launched missiles and tactical nuclear weapons in Europe. Such a commander would have to be pretty determined to push through a successful launch on his own say-so, but, in theory at least, he *could* do it.

Other fears of accidental war center on the stratagems of terrorists or provocateurs, who might choose to trigger a war for their own purposes. The apparent detonation of a nuclear device by an unknown party off the coast of South Africa in late 1979 only emphasizes the difficulty of keeping track of something which might fit comfortably into a steamer trunk. Earlier that year China invaded Vietnam despite stern warnings from Moscow. It is not inconceivable that Moscow might have followed its warnings with action, and that China might have found itself at war with Russia. In such a situation China would hope to get us involved, and we would hope to stay out of it. What better way to force our hand than to simulate a Russian attack on the United States? It sounds farfetched, but it *could* happen. Russia stressed this danger in the first round of SALT talks. People in the Pentagon worry about such possibilities too, and over the years have developed means of establishing whether sudden local disasters are *nuclear* disasters, and what has caused them. In the event we couldn't pinpoint the source we would probably just sit tight, jittery and alert, and wait to see what happened next. Presumably the Russians would do the same. The consequences of impetuosity are too great for any other approach.

Worrying about accidental war makes sense, but it tends to obscure the much greater likelihood of a war beginning in the traditional manner, as the result of a political crisis which no one could find a way to settle. I can't think of a single war which has begun as the result of a genuine accident. Military commanders at sea, or in garrison on distant borders, have always exercised a great deal of local discretion, but I can't think of one who has slipped his mooring and successfully pushed his country into war. Nations often go to war against their better judgment, or with lightheaded disdain for the consequences, but that is not what we mean by accidental. No one wanted war in August 1914, unless it was a handful of Serbian nationalists, but the Great Powers went ahead anyway, when they might have gone back. Even the Second World War was backed into; Hitler was apparently no less surprised by Britain's declaration of war in defense of Poland than Britain was herself. Genuinely deliberate wars seem to be limited to attacks on weak powers by strong powers—Japan's invasion of Manchuria, say, or Italy's of Ethiopia. Generally, Great Powers go to war because they can't think what else to do.

This fact suggests that the extravagant worry over accidental war is really a sign of deep, unconscious fear. Relations between the United States and the Soviet Union are conducted by traditional diplomacy. Both sides have been sober and cautious, for the most part, but they still deal with each other mainly by military gesture, political alliance and verbal warning. It has worked so far, but it is no different from the methods used to maintain the peace during the first half of the century. No one seems able to think of a better approach. The international system, in short, is inherently no more stable than it has been at any other time in the last century or two. Brezhnev is no Hitler, but neither was Kaiser Wilhelm. Worry about accidental war is beside the point, because it does not address the real cause of wars. When the time comes, it won't be a computer that sets things off, but some group of men convinced the other side will back down once they see we mean business.

5. SIGNS OF WAR

I met a woman, some years ago, who had a number tattooed on her forearm. She served coffee in her living room on a kibbutz near the Sea of Galilee. I didn't ask about the number. A relative had sketched in the story. Her family had planned to leave but didn't move quickly enough. History has a way of catching you by surprise. She turned sixteen in Auschwitz. I often think about her when I am talking with my friend R. in New York.

Early in 1980 R. worried that things were slipping out of control. He thought he smelled war in the air. It wasn't just the hostage crisis in Iran, then in the first bloom of impasse, or the Russian invasion of Afghanistan. It was the little stories, some only two or three paragraphs long, which he read in the *Times:* a report of Russian troop concentrations on the northern border of Iran, American fleet movements, the basing of Russian aircraft along the southwestern border of Afghanistan, far from the areas where rebels were active, close to Iran, close to the Gulf. Worst was the story anonymously quoting U.S. military officials to the effect there was little the Americans could do if the Russians decided to move; the choices pretty much came down to acquiescence, or the use of tactical nuclear weapons. My friend R. got a passport and seriously thought of taking his family to New Zealand.

But this isn't the sort of move you can arrange in a day. It is very difficult to tell when a "critical situation"—an arena of danger bristling with chances for war—has reached a point where actual hostilities are imminent. Things which might lead to war usually don't. Things which do can be so inconsequential, at first, they escape notice. Before the shooting starts there is always a chance things might be settled peacefully. After the shooting starts, it's too late. I argued with R. that no one had more than one guess in him. If you guessed wrong and then spent three weeks at great expense cooling your heels in an Auckland hotel you'd never regain the confidence in your own judgment to guess boldly again. Odds are, the next time you'd be too skeptical, too hopeful, and too late. In the event, R. never went beyond getting a passport. He's still thinking about moving to New Zealand permanently, but for the moment is busy with other things. The air has cleared, and he feels safe.

But that leaves the problem of how to tell when a war is about to begin. This is not something which has been much discussed in print. The literature of war concerns itself, for the most part, with military history. The shelves of libraries are groaning with tomes recounting the progress of armies in minute detail. These books, however interesting, always remind me of E. M. Forster's remark that the appeal of novels is the implicit question: and then? and then? Military histories have a similar narrative line: first the generals did this, and then they did that, until finally the generals on one side could do no more. Such histories recount our collective experience of war, but they fail to close with war as a thing, war as a kind of behavior. In the spirit of Clausewitz they treat war as a rational endeavor (even when foolishly conducted)—

the pursuit of policy by other means. They suggest that war becomes increasingly unlikely as sensible men see less and less hope of winning something worth the candle from a recourse to arms. It follows that when there is no hope of success there is no chance of war.

But the history of particular wars is replete with disastrous miscalculations, wars in which high feeling swept away all sense of proportion and restraint, wars blundered into, wars embarked upon in a mood of almost suicidal despondency. The thing which makes war possible is not reason for it, but capacity for it. Wherever we find armies we must assume that in some circumstances they will go to war. But which?

There is not much to be gained by describing all the situations which might lead to war—the mixture of oil and anarchy in the Persian Gulf, say, or the isolation of Berlin, or the great empty place where Russian and Chinese armies stare at each other across a mythical line in the earth—because there are so many of them, because each one is so factually complex, and because such situations offer only a possible occasion for war, without requiring it. There is too much variety and surprise in human affairs for us to predict the moment of war solely by examining in detail the sources of animosity. War is not what comes after the equals sign in an equation. What distinguishes war from peace is a sudden and dramatic increase in willingness to both suffer and inflict injury. Peace is careful, war profligate. The catalytic element, then—the thing one must watch for—is mood, a change in feeling, a conviction the only way out is forward. In our century—and especially in our half of our century— a decision for war must be a desperate thing. If we listen for that note, we may be able to hear war coming.

The theory I'm working from here is that a major war

between great powers will be the result of a kind of self-entrapment. Nations are active creatures; they cannot sit still. When they are big enough to act freely they are continually seeking advantage—a new alliance here, the right to patrol an international strait there, the replacement of a hostile government by a friendly one, exclusive commercial rights, the military embarrassment of opponents with the aid of proxies, the intimidation of neighbors, the secret shipment of arms to the enemies of an opponent's ally, and so on. Peace is not the absence of strife, just strife of a quieter kind—a restless tugging and shoving. But these initiatives always run the risk of being too successful, and thus eliciting a response on a higher level, a kind of raising of the ante. Because power has an intangible side—the qualities of will which lend weight to words, the stuff of prestige—matters of small importance in themselves may loom suddenly large. It is only necessary for one side to insist things are going to be this way, rather than that. Once committed, great powers do not like to back down. Most of the important Cold War crises have been affairs of this sort—the struggle of rivals over matters which would have seemed small, even trivial, if they had not involved questions of intangible will. This suggests that the essence of a war-precipitating crisis is a confrontation in which the possible outcomes progressively narrow to failure, or a step in the direction of war—a raising of the ante—as a sign of determination. It is the sort of thing, on an international scale, which we might describe, if individuals were involved, as getting into a pickle. This seems the most likely way a big general war might begin now, not only because we get about halfway into a pickle every few years, and sometimes oftener, but also because the weapons we have acquired for such a war are so frankly terrifying it is hard to imagine anyone deliberately choosing to use them, until he felt himself back flat up to the wall.

The first stage of a pre-war crisis, then, is closing—the coming together of two sides in a dispute. The point at issue might be one of either actual or symbolic substance. Western access to oil in the Persian Gulf (or Poland's allegiance to the Warsaw Pact) would be an example of the former, Berlin (or Cuba) of the latter. My own feeling is that the relative importance of the point at issue would not be as significant as the fact of closing, accompanied by an atmosphere of crisis.

The second stage would be deadlock—the announcement of mutually conflicting claims. At that point hopes for a peaceful settlement depend on one or both sides surrendering goals in whole or in part. Each side hopes the other will back down first. It is primarily danger that would make one or both sides think twice. This offers a risky opportunity to the more resolute of the two. Determination may carry the day, as it did for the United States over Cuba in 1962, but it also raises the stakes, for the simple reason that backing down gets harder to do (and costs more politically), the longer it is put off.

The third stage would follow the issuance of an ultimatum—a clear and unambiguous warning to the other side not to do something, or to do something. The latter, requiring a positive act, is inherently more provocative. One can always pretend to decline to do something for reasons of one's own. But to *do* something, to walk alone across the stage with the whole world watching . . . ! At this point those thinking about New Zealand would be wise to book passage. An ultimatum is equally hard to accept, and to take back. Issuing an ultimatum serves as an earnest of implacable resolution, but it doesn't leave an opponent much room to maneuver. In the past an ultimatum was often little more than a formality, a kind of prelude to hostilities. In 1962 Kennedy issued an ultimatum to Khrushchev but he was careful to call it by another name, and he made it clear privately he neither wanted war nor intended to exploit a Russian retreat. Even so, war, for a short time, was not far away.

The fourth stage would follow a shot fired in anger. At that point the planes to New Zealand would be filled.

It is entirely possible that all four stages of a war-precipitating crisis might occur in secret, making it difficult for an ordinary reader of newspapers to sense the growing desperation of the situation. Before Kennedy announced his blockade of Cuba in 1962 journalists had only the vaguest sense that something was up, and no sense of its seriousness. Kennedy's advisers at one point favored a surprise attack on the Russian missile sites. If this advice had been accepted, the first sign of war would have been an act of war. Kennedy wisely shrank from so bold an initiative, and it is likely, but not certain, that future crises will follow a similar pattern.

In any event an ordinary citizen might see war coming only if he has a sensitive ear for that note of the desperate characteristic of a government under severe stress. Background stories in the media and wild fluctuations in the financial markets would tell us little. Reports of troop movements, especially those which close forces, would tell us more. But it is the small things which might tell us most. Complete isolation of the president and his main advisers would be an alarming sign, and perhaps the clearest signal of all would be any report of emotional agitation in public by an important official—a cracking voice, trembling hands, an outburst of irrational anger, weeping, etc. Reporters do not mention such things, even in the twentieth paragraph, unless they are dramatic and unmistakable. If I were planning on leaving for New Zealand, that sort of thing would probably send me to the airport.

But I am not at all certain we would see war coming, even if every step towards it were of the sort which in retrospect would appear to be clear, logical, and progressive. For one thing, it is hard to accept the imminence of an event which arouses deep fear. For another, things can happen so quickly. If the distance from the onset of crisis to deadlock were imagined as a mile, the distance from deadlock to ultimatum might be a thousand yards; from ultimatum to a shot fired in anger, 100 yards; from a shot fired in anger to the first use of a nuclear weapon, 10 yards; and from first use of a nuclear weapon to general war, 3 feet. This is only intended to suggest that tension accelerates the process. For those planning on refuge in New Zealand, it might be wise to anticipate—to behave as you would if a crisis had already proceeded to the next stage.

But there are arguments for another approach. When I talk about this with R., I remember the woman with the tattoo on her forearm. Her home in Israel was not far from the Syrian border. The sound of the guns had been clearly audible in 1973. The children of the kibbutz had been moved into a deep shelter covered by a great mass of broken rock held together by several layers of chicken wire. They slept there every night until the war ended. The woman with the tattoo had relatives in Canada; she might have left. But she had already been driven from one home, and did not intend to abandon another. It might be said that she had passed the point where she worried first about herself personally. There is sense in that, too.

6. SPASM WAR

In the fall of 1980, I went to see the deputy undersecretary of defense for strategic and space systems in the Office of the Undersecretary of Defense for Research and Engineering, a man with a crewcut and horn-rimmed glasses named Dr. Seymour Zeiberg. We talked about the MX missile complex which the Air Force wanted to build in an area of central Nevada and Utah called the Great Basin. Dr. Zeiberg is a thoughtful man. He is not unmindful of the dangers of nuclear war, nor immune to moments of gloom. "When I feel like that I get away for a while," he said, "take a ride in an airplane, go out to an Air Force base somewhere and kick a few tires."

Dr. Zeiberg thought the MX was a good idea. I didn't, for reasons which must have been apparent from the questions I asked. During World War II something under three million tons of conventional explosives were dropped by Allied bombers over Europe. The 2000 warheads of the MX system could deliver the equivalent of 700 million tons of conventional explosives. I suppose I must have sounded as if I thought the results would be 200 times worse than the results of WW II. Dr. Zeiberg took a more relaxed view. He thought I had misconceived the probable course of any new war involving the MX or other modern strategic weapons systems. "You're too hung up on spasm war," he said. I've been thinking about this ever since.

"Spasm war" is a phrase popularized by the civilian strategist and defense consultant Herman Kahn. He used it to refer to an all-out, unrestrained, fire-everything war between the United States and the Soviet Union—in effect, a war of annihilation conducted in a mood that might be described as murderous and suicidal in about equal measure. American and Soviet strategic weapons systems are extraordinarily responsive to central direction. A single order by the president could fire all of the 1052 land-based ICBMs within two or three minutes. It would take somewhat longer to fire the SLBMs from nuclear submarines because of communications difficulties. Nuclear weapons carried by conventional aircraft would take the longest of all, but even so the United States *could* deliver just about all of its warheads in less than twelve hours. The Soviets could do the same. This is what Kahn was referring to in the first instance—a brief, instinctive, unrestrained assault that would doubtless bring the same in return.

Dr. Zeiberg considers a spasm war very unlikely. Its consequences would of course be catastrophic, something well understood by the political leaders and military men of both sides. Even a first strike—that is, a Pearl Harbor type of surprise attack on military targets—would probably be limited in the hope of mitigating the response. But the real point at issue here is not whether a substantial majority of our strategic weapons will be fired on the first day (a spasm war in its archetypal form), but whether the war will continue until they are pretty much used up. We might describe the latter as a spasmodic war—a succession of salvos, one wave of attacks eliciting another in response, as each side tried to bend the other to its will.

In some respects this might be even worse than an all-out war, over in a day, if only because initial recovery efforts —the establishment of new hospitals, transportation centers, emergency tent cities, military rendezvous points, and the like—would offer new targets for attack.

The truth of the matter is that Dr. Zeiberg, like just about every other professional defense expert, does not expect any sort of nuclear exchange, ever—much less a spasm war—between the United States and the Soviet Union. If we can maintain at least a rough balance of forces then we can avoid war. This is why Dr. Zeiberg favors the MX. Like the rest of the defense community, he feels the best we can hope for is a Mexican stand-off.

But even if a war should begin—he does not know how this might happen, and neither do I—Dr. Zeiberg thinks both sides would agree to call a halt in the war's early stages, not go all the way. I take the opposite view, and ever since our conversation I have been trying to figure out why.

Let me begin with a confession: I have no direct, personal experience of war. I never set foot in Vietnam. Once, in the biblical city of Tyre on the coast of southern Lebanon, a friend and I thought we heard artillery in the distance, but it was only a single, isolated boom in the night. Some years earlier, in Athens the night of the colonels' coup in 1967, my wife and I sat up late on a pleasant terrace, listening to occasional bursts of machine-gun fire and wondering what was happening. Apparently very little; there were no reports of casualties the following day. Nor have I been in government—or in any large institution, for that matter—at a moment of crisis. Tolstoy once said that anyone who has seen a street fight can understand a great battle. Whatever knowledge I have of war is of that sort, or comes from reading and from thinking about what I have read. The result is a notion of war quite different from that of Dr. Zeiberg.

Most writing about war treats it as the solution to a problem—the rational (albeit dangerous) pursuit of a tangible (albeit arguable) goal. But this does not explain why so many possible occasions for war are passed up, nor why the fighting is so hard to stop once begun. Clearly war has its rational side, but this is limited to the mechanics of military operations. It is like chess in more ways than one; the way it is played determines who will win, but has nothing to do with the larger question—why the game is undertaken in the first place. So it is with war. The techniques of combat reveal little about the spirit of war, which exists on a different plane. That spirit is not easy to put down.

Perhaps the first thing to be said of big modern wars —and in particular of the two great wars of our century —is that their violence has been dramatically out of proportion to their original goals. The First World War began in a hopeless muddle of aims—the confused desire, on both sides, to emerge from a conflict of will over a trivial matter with that enhancement of prestige, that aura of confident strength, which comes from getting your way with everybody watching. Either side might have backed down without an iota of diminishment of tangible strength. The same might be said of the conflict over Poland in 1939. The fate of neither Poland nor the Balkans can plausibly be said to have justified the immense suffering, death, and destruction of the wars for which they served as occasion.

An occasion is just that—a moment for beginning, not a reason for carrying on to the end. Once the belligerents have joined in combat the occasion fades in significance and the struggle itself becomes paramount. (Clausewitz defines the object of military operations as destruction of the enemy's capacity to fight. Once that is achieved all else follows. The victor has the luxury of deciding what the war was about after it is over.

But in modern wars the prize—territory, reparations, access to material resources—is dwarfed by the cost of winning it. The real object of war seems to be something quite different, an end to the threat posed by hostile arms. In theory arms are acquired in order to defend something one has got, but arms cannot defend without threatening. Arms, in short, are both cause and result of arms. It is tough enough to live in fear of arms in peacetime. In war the threat becomes actual, and is more than the spirit can bear. Thus a war which might begin over something small—a bullying reply to a diplomatic note; title to a chunk of Central Europe—tends toward an open-ended struggle to free oneself from the threat of arms by destroying them. When whole societies have been devoted to preparation for war we can expect conflict to be on a commensurate scale. About the only thing one might hope to gain from such a war is freedom from the fear of having to go through it again. The oil of the Persian Gulf might serve as an occasion for war between the United States and the Soviet Union, but that isn't what it would be *about*. In war ontology is everything. Their beginnings have one kind of logic, their ends another. It is weapons which threaten us, and weapons which we fight to destroy. We might say that the reason wars are fought —as opposed to the reason they begin—is to see who will be left with weapons at the end.

The second thing we might say about big modern wars is they do not end when one side surrenders, but when one side is beaten. During the First World War Bertrand Russell was briefly sent to jail for having suggested that

the war couldn't possibly win anything worth the sacrifice involved, and that it ought to be ended immediately
on any terms available. This was a sensible suggestion.
The four great belligerents—Britain, France, Russia, and
Germany—all but destroyed themselves for what
amounted in the end to illusory reparations, an illusory
hegemony in Europe, minor colonial acquisitions, and
inconsequential changes in European frontiers. Russia, of
course, gained nothing at all—not even illusions. In terms
of money, the war was merely ruinous. In terms of life,
it beggared the horrors of history. Whole generations of
young men were cut in half. Thus began the darkening
of the modern mind. But with all these excellent reasons
for halting the war in mid-battle, no leader on either side
ever seriously suggested doing so. Even at the very end
the Germans could not bring themselves to surrender, but
dithered until a revolution at home settled the matter.

The Second World War was even more replete with
opportunities for surrender. No one did so. Even France
waited until it was clear its army was incapable of fighting
before accepting an armistice. Britain had no hope of
winning in June, 1940, but she did not surrender. Russia
seemed all but beaten in the late summer of 1941, but did
not surrender. Germany and Japan were both beaten by
the end of 1944. Neither surrendered. The losers were
beaten—hammered down until they could fight no
longer. The logic of war seems to be that if a belligerent
can fight he will fight, that leaders will not surrender until
surrender is academic. This appears to be a corollary of
the immense cost of modern war. Victory may be ashes,
but at least it is *something*. How is a national leader to
explain the sacrifice of so much for *nothing*? It is more
than they can bring themselves to do. The loss of cities

and armies is not taken as reason for quitting, but as reason for risking the rest.

The military is asked, Must we surrender today? The military answers, No, not today, we are not beaten yet. Time foreshortens terribly. The psychology is that of the man condemned to be hanged, described by Dostoevsky. It is the moment the condemned man dreads. *Not yet*, he tells himself the night before his last day. *Not yet*, he says in the morning. *Not yet*, as he is led to the door. *Not yet*, as he reaches the stair to the scaffold. *Not yet*, when there is still one step to climb. A man does not have to die until the noose draws tight. A nation does not have to surrender until it is beaten. The awful cost of war is reason to shrink back before it begins; afterwards, it serves as goad.

The third major characteristic of big wars in our century has been their level of gratuitous destruction. The ghastly loss of life in combat during the First World War was not repeated in the Second, but civilian casualties increased enormously. Big Bertha, the huge German railroad gun which fired on Paris in 1918, scared more people than it injured. Civilian bombardment in WWII was on an altogether different scale. Whole cities were destroyed in an attempt to break civilian morale. The approach did not work. The practical reasons for strategic bombing, as it was called, were two: air defenses were too effective by day, and cities were the only targets big enough to find at night. But the infliction of pain on this scale is hard to understand as anything except a response to anger, suffering, and frustration—all of which are in the nature of war. Nuclear weapons, of course, offer an ideal means for inflicting pain. Cities are the one target that cannot become lost in the confusion of war. We might sum up, then, by saying that big modern wars are violent out of all proportion to goals, are fought to the bitter end, and encourage gratuitous destruction.

What does this suggest about the course of a war between the United States and the Soviet Union? Both sides are armed, and threaten each other, beyond all precedent. The cost would be great from the opening shot. Other belligerents—especially China and West Germany—might enter the war at an early stage. The United States assumes it would lose a conventional war without recourse to nuclear weapons. We may take it as a given that the occasion for war would be a substantial one—access to oil in the Persian Gulf, perhaps. We may assume that one side had committed itself to X, and the other to resisting X. Could either side lightly drop its commitment once the shooting started? Would either side be in a mood for compromise once the shooting had already cost more than X was worth?

It is possible that one side or the other, reading the logic of the situation in a cold light, would abandon all restraint and reach for whatever advantage is to be obtained from a sudden, spasmic firing of everything in its arsenal. But this strikes me as unlikely. In my imagination—and at this point imagination is all any of us has to go on—the war follows a different course. One act of destruction elicits another. Fleets and armies are destroyed. Panic spreads, communications are strained, confusion rises. Things happen quickly; there is no time to think. The leaders of neither side can bear to have lost so much for *nothing*. And yet the horror is all contained in messages on bits of paper. The loss of an entire city, unimaginable before the war, still leaves many others. The war does not *have* to end now.

The arsenals we have built are very great. Once the war had begun in earnest—once we had truly begun to suffer

—it seems to me the shooting would continue in spasmodic waves until technological exhaustion asserted itself, and we could no longer get at each other. What else are those weapons *for?* But as I say, Dr. Zeiberg thinks otherwise, and God willing, he'll turn out to be right.

7. AFTER THE BOMBS

In 1975 the National Academy of Sciences published a long, interesting, technically detailed study which is well-described by its title: *Long Term Worldwide Effects of Multiple Nuclear Weapons Detonations.* This is a book which demands to be read slowly, especially by scientific laymen. It concludes the effects would be grim, of course, but not apocalyptic. Senator Richard Russell once said that if mankind had to start over, he hoped the new Adam would be an American. He was exaggerating. The planet would not be rendered lifeless by a general war, nor even the Northern Hemisphere where most of the warheads could be expected to detonate. In short, there would be a postwar world. People would survive in numbers to reflect on the past and plan for the future. Much of the infrastructure of industrial civilization would survive too. The landmass of North America would be organized into one or more nation states, just as it is now. This would also be the case in Eurasia. What would be the defense policies of these postwar states?

Last summer I asked this question of a couple of academic defense specialists while we were eating healthy lunches in a salad bar in Cambridge. Lettuce, bean sprouts, endive, watercress, chick peas, a dozen kinds of relish, the works. It is a curious fact that gloomy subjects can actually enhance the appetite. They didn't know the answer. I didn't either. One of them, a young physicist who had been prodded into defense policy by knowledge of what bombs do, said he found such a war unthinkable, his imagination could not carry him beyond the outbreak of hostilities. "My mind just stops there," he said. His study of the subject had convinced him it just *can't* happen. Not in the sense that objects can't fall up, spring can't follow summer, two and two can't equal five, a man can't breathe underwater, but in the sense that a father can't kill his own child.

But of course a father can kill his own child. A free hour in the morning and a subscription to the *New York Times* are all we need to know that distressing things happen with appalling frequency in this world. A nuclear war might happen too. There is no question we have been preparing for one at great expense over the last thirty-five years, and we are about to embark upon a whole new round of weapons-building to ensure the Russians know we can respond in kind to anything they might choose to throw our way.

The progress of arms has a glacial quality to it, not in terms of speed—the building has been quite brisk, considered over the long haul—but in terms of fateful inexorability. It is hard to think of a year which has not left us with better, more numerous, more powerful, more accurate arms. But theories for their use come in fits and starts. The first nuclear weapons were a kind of mighty hammer, vast in power but hard to aim accurately. Now missiles can be dropped right down into Yankee Stadium from the other side of the planet. The defense professionals who came to power with President Reagan have a new theory that war can best be prevented by a demonstrable capacity to fight one to the finish if it should occur. Perhaps they are right. One thing is certain: the new theory demands a lot of new hardware, and it is going to be expensive.

It is not war we shall be talking about over the next year or two, but the cost of weapons—things like a new manned bomber, a superaccurate new land-based missile which can be hidden from Russian surprise attack, the revival of plans for an anti-ballistic missile system. President Kennedy arrived in Washington with a similar program for beefing up U.S. strategic weaponry in 1961, and in short order doubled the defense budget. We can expect the same again. Reagan has promised to compensate for these new expenditures by cuts in other federal programs, but odds are this will prove hard to do, as it always has in the past. If deficits in federal spending have anything to do with inflation, the combination of tax cuts and new arms spending in Reagan's program is going to mean a lot of inflation. But that is a side issue.

The real issue, as always, is war. This is hard to think about clearly. In Washington people don't think about war, but about defense. For officials, defense means deciding how much to spend on what. Such severely practical thinking never looks much further into the future than next year's budget. Intelligence projections of Soviet military capacity ten years down the road are considered to be on the furthermost horizon of the human capacity to foresee what lies ahead; and indeed, those projections have often been wrong. Responsibility has a foreshortening effect; the effort to decide what to *do* seems to put all but convinced pacifists firmly in the camp of the weapons-builders. Some like one system, some another. So long as the other side is building weapons—and it is—we have got to respond somehow. Thus the argument goes.

But there is another possible approach to these matters.

If one simply refuses the whole question of what to do, in the manner of a horse refusing a jump, then the pattern of the last thirty-five years takes on a certain clarity. It looks like one of preparation for war to me. But maybe I'm wrong. For the sake of argument alone, then, let's assume for the moment such a war has taken place, that the destruction and loss of life have been extensive but not universal, and that the shooting has now stopped. What can we say about the geopolitical facts of life in the post-war world? I can think of six things which are likely.

(1) Neither the United States nor the Soviet Union would have the capacity to occupy the other side. Decisive wars tend to end with the collapse of one belligerent. In the final stages the loser's army disintegrates, surrenders in chunks, runs out of munitions as transportation breaks down, or just melts away. This enables the victor to dictate a peace. At the end of both World Wars the Allies had more than strength enough to deal with Germany as they liked. A major nuclear war would bleed both sides white, not necessarily in exactly equal measure, but more than enough to rule out the possibility of the huge logistical effort involved in occupying a continental power at the far side of an ocean. It is occupation of that sort—not battle—which completes destruction of an enemy's military capacity. This is what is meant—or what ought to be meant—when it is said that in nuclear war there can be no winners. As a practical matter, each of the two sides would be in control of its own recovery.

(2) The shooting would stop before either side had fired off everything in its nuclear inventory. A kind of Zeno's paradox would probably be in effect. It is accepted military practice always to hold something in reserve, which suggests that no salvo would use more than half or at most three-quarters of what was available. The war might drag

on for months or even years, but something would always be left. The Russian and American economies might be reduced to a nineteenth-century scale by the fighting, but a certain number of twentieth-century weapons would remain. As a result, each side would continue to threaten the other, thus establishing an important psychological link to strategic thinking in the pre-war world. The scale of confrontation would have changed, but not its nature.

(3) Of all the institutions which make up American society, the one best organized to survive both the war itself and the stress, danger, and privation of the postwar world would probably be the military. The creation of a new central authority would depend heavily on military communications and transportation, and no other institution would have the strength to enforce the harsh measures necessary to suppress looters and allocate scarce resources in a time of possible plague, cold, and famine. The military would inevitably become the locus of order. It is even possible that the military would itself run the country for a time.

But whatever domestic political arrangements emerged in the postwar world, it is hard to imagine that the influence of the military—and of military approaches to geopolitical problems—would be less than they are now, which is very great. In the Soviet Union the Communist party, an almost equally self-contained institution, would probably survive along with the military. If this is true, the very elements on both sides which tended to be most suspicious of each other before the war, would probably find their postwar roles actually enhanced, however disastrous the war itself might be.

(4) No one would know how the war began. If it emerged from an international crisis, as seems likely, the general events preceding the outbreak of hostilities would

be known, but the precise moment and reasons it turned nuclear would be obscure. The reason for this is that the White House, the Pentagon, the CIA, the National Security Agency which monitors broadcasts, the headquarters of the Strategic Air Command in Omaha, and other sites which the military refers to as "nodes" of communications, command, control, and intelligence (sometimes written in the literature as "C^3I") would all be prime targets in a major nuclear war. The same would be true in Russia. The blame for a nuclear war would rest most heavily on the side which first resorted to nuclear weapons. Not knowing with any certainty who that was— since those responsible would be mostly dead, and the records mostly destroyed—both sides would be at liberty to blame the other for the disaster. Perhaps this is a small point.

(5) A nuclear war would give the United States and Russia their first real cause for mutual hatred. As nations we are already quite hostile despite the fact we have never really damaged or injured each other. The damage and injury of a nuclear war would of course be on a heroic scale, the sort of thing which sinks deep as myth into the popular mind, and stays there. Hatred isn't the only thing responsible for hostility between nations, but it certainly helps. It is the same with suspicion.

Anxiety about nuclear war at the moment is like a low-grade fever—a persistent, troubling, half-conscious mix of fear and worry which is rarely articulated. Most people, and especially those professionally involved in major questions of defense, don't really believe war is likely, or that it would slip out of control. This time, they seem to think, everyone will come to his senses at the very latest by September 1914. An actual war would naturally change all that. In a postwar world both sides would have substantial cause for hatred, and would know, not merely suspect, that the other was morally capable of assault on a genocidal scale. Relations now conducted in a spirit of wary but hopeful caution would be—if they resumed at all—cold and bitter, touched by violent antipathy, and very likely marked by a heartfelt desire for the other's annihilation, if it could only be encompassed.

(6) Both sides would have only the sketchiest knowledge of the military, economic, and political conditions of the other. It is tough enough to find out what the Soviets are up to now, when normal commercial and diplomatic relations provide broad general knowledge, which is backed up by elaborate (but vulnerable) means of technical surveillance. All such facilities would be early targets in a general war, leaving both sides in a great postwar dark. The two sides *might* retain some knowledge of what they had fired at, but at best could only guess at the results.

In a postwar world there would be no way of knowing whether the other side was worse off, about the same, or even—horrors of horrors—relatively unscathed. Perhaps the Tallinn line really was an ABM system, and it worked. Perhaps their civil defense efforts were even more effective than we'd feared. Perhaps our own missiles weren't as accurate as we'd hoped. Perhaps the attrition rate of our bombers and cruise missiles was really ninety-five percent, instead of just thirty or forty. There would be no way for us to know, and, severely damaged, fearing a resumption of the war, we would probably do what we have always done in the past where exact knowledge was lacking—assume the worst.

What do these conjectures add up to? The picture strikes me as a gloomy one: no winner, at least some strategic weapons retained by both sides, an enhanced or even preeminent role for the military, a tendency to blame the other side for the disaster, real cause for hatred and suspicion, less knowledge than ever of what the other side was planning or doing. It is difficult to avoid the conclusion that the most probable result of a general nuclear war would be a race to recover economic and military strength in order to be ready for a second general nuclear war.

But of course this is all purely speculative.

8. WHAT TO TELL
THE KIDS

"I got you!"
"You missed!"
"No, I didn't! You're dead!"

That's the way it went in cops and robbers, or cowboys and Indians, or war. I can still remember a lot of the toy guns I had as a kid—a double-barreled cap-firing pirate pistol, a German Luger cast in silvery pot metal and painted black, a big six-shooter with actual cartridges, a tommy gun with a drum clip of the sort Chicago gangsters used in the movies. I had toy soldiers, played war with my friends, drew war pictures in school when I should have been studying. In the attic were cartons of old *Life* magazines from the 1940s. I spent hours poring over the World War II pictures on rainy afternoons. One photo particularly sticks in my mind—of a Japanese skull on a tank in the Pacific. The flesh had dried down tight like wrinkled leather and the mouth was open in a scream of anguish. That picture gave me a sort of shivery feeling, but I can't say that it really scared me.

War was very much part of my imaginative life when I was ten or twelve, in the early 1950s. There was a room in the cellar with a moderate stock of canned goods, bottled water, and a Sterno stove. That was "in case." I can remember waiting my turn in the barbershop and

reading a copy of *Police Gazette* containing two stories of
equal fascination—the positive identification of Hitler in
Argentina, where he was living as a retired businessman,
and the Red Army's timetable for the invasion of Europe.
War was exciting and mysterious, like Flying Saucers or
the Loch Ness Monster. I remember the day the war in
Korea began. It came over the radio. My father was serious, alert, tense, and eager to explain what everything
meant. For the next couple of years I read about Korea
in comic books. In the summer, in Vermont, I used to go
hunting woodchucks with the .22 rifle my grandfather
had given me. But my real targets were Chinese soldiers
wearing padded uniforms and "Chicoms"—the quilted
cotton hats with earflaps which tied up over the top of the
head. They had infiltrated down through Canada to in-
vade the United States. I knew this was ridiculous, but
how else was I to get the game going?

I was quite conscious of the Russians as a dangerous
horde. I must have heard about the "captive nations" but
it didn't register. Their very names—Poland, Rumania,
Bulgaria, Czechoslovakia—had a sinister sound. I thought
of those places as being part of Russia. No one ever sat
me down in a class, or at home, and explained things to
me. I had no idea what this was all about. War seemed
part of the natural order of things. Communism was a
secret movement of malevolent intent. The other side was
waiting its chance. It was only a matter of time before
another big war got going.

But for some reason none of this frightened me. We
had air raid drills in school but it was kind of a joke. We
lined up and marched out into the corridors, sat down on
the floor backs to the wall, and put our heads down
between our knees. This seems to be a common memory
among people who were children at that time. War was

in the air, but I had a child's sense of time. Eons passed between one birthday and another. I believed it would all be over by the time I grew up. It was like cancer. "They" would have found a cure by the time I was old enough to get it. Perhaps the fact I played war made me think of it as only a game.

Now things are quite different. War worries me a great deal, I have three daughters of my own, and I wonder what to tell them. One day last summer the oldest, Amanda, asked me what my book was about. I am asked this all the time. It's a form of polite inquiry. People don't mean anything by it. You ask brokers how the market is going, you ask the old how they're feeling, you ask farmers what they think of the sky, and you ask writers what they're working on. I'm working on a book about strategic weapons. How interesting, people say. That's very topical just now. You'd better get it out soon while everybody's still interested. This remark, which has popped spontaneously from more people than you would imagine, used to fill me with despair. It made the job seem hopeless. How can a writer pierce a carapace so thick?

But of course piercing that carapace is precisely the point of the undertaking. I think about this a lot and try out my stratagems on the unwary. If there's time, and we're not just glancing off each other on the street or at a party—in short, when I've got someone in a corner for fifteen or twenty minutes—I can usually scare the living daylights out of them. But what do I tell my daughters, who are four, nine, and eleven? Do I want to scare them? Can fear possibly do them any good? How can children live with a knowledge of the world as it really is when adults find it so difficult? Wouldn't it be better to brush by the question with some short, neutral answer—"it's about the Air Force," say—and let it go?

Words have an extraordinary power with children, especially vivid, concrete words. My youngest daughter likes the story of Little Red Riding Hood. She likes the scary parts, but not if they're too scary. One night I overdid it. When we got to the part about the wolf I lingered on the powerful jaws and the teeth—with the long sharp biters in front and the big grinders in back. She clapped her hand over my mouth. "Don't, Dad," she said. "You're scaring me! Don't talk about the teeth!"

Adults are practiced in denial, but children are defenseless. Once something is vivid in their minds, it's right there in the room. My father, who is now eighty-nine, once described to me his earliest memory. He was only two or three at the time. He was living with his grandfather in Owensboro, Kentucky, in a big old Victorian house. Around the yard in front was a picket fence. One day my father was out in the yard with his dog. A man was walking by on the sidewalk. He stopped near my father, took out his pocket knife, opened it, bent down over the picket fence, and in a low deliberate voice stressing each word he said, *"I'm going to cut your ears off!"*

That happened eighty-seven years ago. My father can describe it now as if it were before his eyes, with every detail burningly vivid. I don't *want* to tell my children what nuclear war would do to them. I don't want them dreaming about it. I don't want them burdened with terrifying images that never fade. They need to grow up first, and get some practice in ignoring things they can't do anything about. They need to learn to hear without hearing, as adults do.

Children are quick at getting the point. Once their curiosity has been aroused they are relentless in pursuing the full story. They sense where you're vulnerable. My two elder daughters once cornered me on the subject of

Santa Claus. "Tell me the truth," said Amanda. "I'll believe whatever you tell me. Is there a Santa Claus or isn't there?" It's hard to see how she could have framed the question more narrowly.

A couple of years earlier she went through a period of wondering about death. She was four or five at the time. Once, when I was giving her a bath, she suddenly said, "I don't want to have to die." I didn't quite get her drift. I explained that everybody dies, we get to live a long time and have lots of experiences but eventually we get old, dying is something we're strong enough to go through, etc. etc. But she interrupted me. She didn't think I was trying to fudge it. I'd simply missed her point. It wasn't the pain of it that troubled her. "It isn't that, Dad," she said. "I don't mind if I get sick, if it just happens. But I don't want to *have* to die."

When my youngest daughter Cassandra turned four she started wondering about death too. One night, when we were alone in the living room, she asked me if everybody dies. I told her the same thing I'd told her sister, wondering what it is about the age of four. She was lying on her back on the couch, waggling her legs in the air, seeming to pay no attention. But when I finished she moved her legs aside and looked me right in the eye and said, "Do they rose after they die?" I was completely caught off guard. I saw the flower in my mind. This exchange took place in April; it must have been talk in Sunday school about Easter which brought on the question. She explained: "Jesus rose so we get to rose, isn't that right, Dad? Everybody gets to rose. Will I rose?" I said this was a hard question to answer. I didn't think so but people in the church *did* think so. "Are we in the church?" I said we're *members* of the church. "But are we *in* the church?"

This is a verbatim transcript. The italics were hers. Children get the point. I have a dread of being pinned down in a similar manner where my book is concerned. That is, where the subject of nuclear weapons is concerned. Specifically, what do these weapons do? Is there any defense against them? Is it going to happen? I can't help what I think but I don't talk about this around the house. Perhaps it's silly. Perhaps they don't really see things any more clearly than I did back in the early 1950s. But when other people bring up this subject when my kids are around, as visitors sometimes do, I grow acutely uneasy. I try to change the subject, or skate over the details. I grow irritable. Don't they notice *kids* are around? Don't they realize that there are some things you just don't tell kids?

In Israel, in 1975, I met a woman with a child who was terrified of war. I can no longer remember if the child was a boy or a girl. I think it was a boy. In his experience war was something which came in the middle of the night, you never knew when. In October, 1973, the child was hustled out of bed to an air raid shelter in the middle of the night. In the morning his father was gone and he was gone a long time. The mother often wept and said the father would be all right, he would be all right. When the boy finally saw his father again, many months later, the father was sitting in a chair on the lawn in front of a military hospital, and there was a blanket over the father's lap. He did not get up. When the mother and the boy left, his father was still sitting on the chair, waving goodbye. Often the boy woke up at night crying. Once when he was in the car with his mother he asked, "What will we do if there's a raid? Where will we hide?" He didn't want to go in the car anymore. He put off going to bed at night. He was afraid he might not hear the sirens if he was asleep. He was afraid of the sounds of airplanes. His mother tried to explain everything but explaining was not enough.

This is what troubles me. War is more than kids can handle. Adults have learned to live with things they can do nothing about. Adults tell themselves people will be sensible. Adults bury things and forget they are there, or think about something else, or busy themselves with earning a living, or put their trust in officials who are paid to worry about these matters, or say it will all work out in the end.

But kids get the point anyway. They pick things up. They don't really need to be told. Maybe I got the point too, back in the early 1950s. Maybe it's not worth worrying about, one of those things you can't help. One day last January, when I was trying to write a piece about the world after a nuclear war, I got stumped. Certain details weren't quite clear to me. My daughter Susan was in the room drawing a picture. Without thinking, I asked her what she thought a war would be like. It just popped out. She answered as if she'd been thinking a long time what to say and I wrote it down. She said, "It would probably be very smoky, and not many people, and lots of things ruined, and dark."

9. DOWN THE
MIRACLE MILE

Tullahoma, Tennessee, is hard to find. It isn't really there anymore. Once upon a time there was a downtown with a courthouse, a post office, churches, a hotel, restaurants, a mainstreet with redbrick buildings and stores on the ground floor—a small city like many others in rural America. Farmers came to town on Saturdays, old men sat on benches, you could walk from any part of town to any other part in ten or fifteen minutes. I don't know if there was a railroad; I certainly didn't see anything like a train station when I drove through one evening in October 1980, looking for a place to have dinner.

The car changed everything. There are gaps in mainstreet now, a lot of the old stores are empty and the ones which remain are sleepy establishments, thin on inventory, tended by unhurried men and women who seem a bit surprised to hear the screen door creak and slam. I was looking for the sort of place where you might sit in a wooden booth, the seat backs rubbed blond, and order a ham steak. I ought to have known better. A handful of storefronts had been modernized back in the 1950s, but it hadn't worked. Business had all moved away to the shopping centers. I stopped at a liquor store surrounded by an asphalt parking lot to ask for a restaurant. I'd say it was on the outskirts of town, but there wasn't really any town anymore. The liquor store was just where it was, at the corner of two streets. It was a one-story affair with a flat roof, plate glass windows in aluminum frames, a counter topped with Formica, the sort of display stands—paperboard printed to look like wood—distributed by the big California wine companies. The woman in the store answered my question with a long list of franchise restaurants—Burger King, McDonald's, Sirloin Pit, and so on. I headed out the road she suggested and there they were, squares of tarmac surrounding one-story buildings of stucco and plywood in what must have been some farmer's field ten or fifteen years ago. There was no discernible pattern. One was plunked down every little way. It was where it was, and that was about all you could say about where it was. Tullahoma isn't there any more. I picked a place and had dinner and don't recommend it. Then I drove back to my motel, a good twenty or thirty miles away on the far side of the Arnold Engineering Development Center (AEDC) where the Air Force tests aircraft, missiles, rocket motors, and such.

The AEDC is the sort of place best seen from a small plane. It's on the site of an old Army post, but that isn't the reason it's there instead of some place else. I'm not sure what the reason is. Maybe it's political. The center covers 44,000 acres, most of it flat woodland. The rest, about 2600 acres, is fenced. The deer inside the fence are fat and tame. A 4000-acre lake is used for cooling purposes. The biggest of the rocket motor test cells uses 500,000 gallons of water *per minute* to cool the exhaust when motors are being fired. These are what the Air Force refers to as "gee whiz" figures. The noise, I was told, is awesome. In addition to water the AEDC uses a lot of power, $20 million worth a year. Some of the big air compressors for wind tunnel tests require 100,000 horsepower. The power drain is so great that most tests are conducted at night.

There's a lot of construction work going on at the AEDC now, some of it gearing up for tests of the new MX missile, but most of it for the new Aeropropulsion Systems Test Facility. The ASTF is budgeted at $437 million, but inflation is probably pushing up the cost. Everything about the AEDC has the look of the big, the ambitious, and the expensive. I talked to a couple of engineers with long histories in defense work and they all seemed intelligent, articulate, cautious, and highly disciplined men. In addition to their work they worry a good deal about the Russians. Until the ASTF is completed the biggest Russian test facility will be about twice as big as the AEDC. The engineers can't understand how we let the Russians get ahead of us in this manner. One man described a series of tests on the Minuteman III ICBM, the backbone of the U.S. missile inventory, to determine its shelf life. Some of the Minutemen are twenty years old, but it turns out they're as good as new. The engineer dropped his caution for a moment and said, with sharp, evident passion: "You can tell that to the Russians!"

The AEDC is impressive, in the literal sense. One knows the military goes about things in a large, comprehensive way, but one is impressed all the same by a testing chamber in a wind tunnel, for example, with a door three or four stories high. Even the hinges, way up there, seemed the size of a Volkswagen bug. I tried to imagine what it sounded like closing. But small things can be impressive too. One was a nose cone for the tips of re-entry vehicles (RVs) which heat up enormously and take a terrific battering from dust and ice crystals as they roar back into the atmosphere at 10,000 miles per hour, carrying a nuclear warhead to some target on the surface of the earth. The nose is round, about the size of a baseball cut in half. If it were pinpoint sharp it would melt. The trick is to make the nose out of some material which will wear away—"ablate"—in a smooth and regular manner in order to minimize the flight perturbations which might edge it off target. All sorts of noses have been tested in a dust erosion tunnel where they are bombarded with magnesium oxide or aluminum oxide in dust-sized particles— about 200 microns across—at 3200 feet per second. Larger grains of about 650 microns, roughly the size of beach sand, simulate what is called a "nuclear environment"— the debris-filled air left by the detonation of a preceding warhead. Before the tests they are as shiny as stainless steel. After the tests they are gun-metal gray, about as rough to the touch as 120 sandpaper. A distinct ring, blue-gray to violet in color, about three inches in diameter, centers on the tip of the nose. This ring is where the heat of re-entry reaches its maximum temperature. If you look closely you can see gradations in the color; there is even a delicate line, thin as a horsehair, almost magenta in hue. Something about this re-entry ring suggests—or it did to me, at least—the awesome, tearing approach of a warhead. It probably cost something on the order of a zillion dollars to bring the art of metallurgy to this level, all so the MX will be able to place warheads within a couple of hundred feet of two intersecting lines on a map of the Russian heartland.

But outside the gates of the AEDC one returns to the Miracle Mile of motels, shopping centers, and fast-food franchise restaurants. This seems to be characteristic of military bases. They're all flat, everybody speaks with a faintly Southern accent, everything is always a long way from everything else, something very large and expensive is going on, and outside the gates the Miracle Mile begins.

Most Americans never see a man in uniform. In Europe they're to be found on every street corner, but Americans have little sense of the size of our military establishment because the bases are all out in some flat, isolated part of the country. Sometimes I think about this while waiting for the Seventh Avenue IRT subway in New York. Believe me, it's getting to be a long wait. When the train comes the windows are a sulphurous yellow with dirt, the lights in the car flicker, people are packed in to bursting. The New York City subway system really and truly is breaking down, starved for money. In February 1981, President Reagan presented his program for cuts in eighty-three domestic programs. By 1986 he proposed to "save"—we shall consider that word *save* in a moment— a total of $13.4 billion from mass-transit programs alone. The total for the first two years would be $40 billion, with more to follow. The cuts were naturally described as reductions in "waste" or "frills" we couldn't really afford. There was much slighting talk of liberal attempts to "throw money at problems," but no talk of the problems. It is fair to conclude Reagan has no plans to throw anything at the problems. The eighty-three programs which Reagan planned to cut cover the entire range of federal programs to support the health and welfare—in the broadest sense—of the American people. They had been enacted over a period of decades, frequently after long debate, and they touch every aspect of American life, from basic scientific research to the arts and agriculture.

The magnitude of Reagan's program is hard to grasp. It would take a serious student weeks to get an idea of what the cuts in any one program really mean. The idea that the Congress could seriously consider all of them, in a single package, within a matter of weeks as the administration insisted it do, is absurd. By 1986, for example, a total of $23 billion in various forms of student loans and assistance will have been scrapped. That would be enough to provide 1.15 million students with $5000 a year for the four years of an undergraduate education. Who would provide those funds—much of them in the form of loans—if Reagan's proposed cuts were accepted? This represents only two programs. After a wise and balanced decision had been reached about them, Congress still had eighty-one left to consider.

Curious what Reagan's proposed cuts would add up to by 1986, I went down the list with my calculator and totted them up. No one else seems to have done this. At any rate I haven't seen the total figure anywhere else. It's a boring job. The grand total—funds which will not be spent on the poor, on transportation, on education, on the exploration of space, on scientific and medical research—is $321.6 billion. This is a very large sum. It represents about a third of the total value of all the companies listed on the New York Stock Exchange. That is a major investment. Doubtless there is waste in the federal budget. There is waste in my budget. But $321.6 billion worth of waste? This is not an exercise in economy, but a broad conclusion that all these undertakings just aren't worth the money.

At this point you might ask what is worth the money? Reagan's answer is: the military—more military and civilian personnel at higher pay, a boost of the Navy from 450 to 600 ships, a new strategic bomber, a new strategic missile system, hundreds of new aircraft of all types, more tanks, research into esoteric new weapons systems like charged particle beams, beefing up the Rapid Deployment Force, expansion of the inventory of munitions of all kinds. The administration has not been eager to spell out the military programs it is planning to fund with all the money cut from domestic spending, for obvious reasons. To a degree, one has to read between the lines. The drift is clear enough—an increase of $33 billion in the first two years, growth in the projected budget to $367 billion in 1985. What Reagan is proposing is a breathtakingly direct trade—social programs for military programs, not a "saving" of $321.6 billion, but its reallocation pure and simple, along with the borrowing of many additional billions to make up the projected deficit. If Reagan gets only the defense half of his program—new military spending, without cuts to match—he will wreck the nation's economy. If he gets both, he will wreck the nation.

It is natural, in situations of this sort, to assume a compromise will be reached—*some* budget cuts in exchange for *some* new military spending. The boldness of Reagan's plan, however, made such a trade-off difficult. In 1981 he got pretty much everything he asked. In 1982, Congress appeared to dig in its heels, frightened by the prospect of $100-billion deficits. But even a compromise on Reagan's second budget would involve huge budget cuts, more than matched by huge increases in military spending. It was the size of the reallocation that was in dispute the second time around, not its necessity. But the real question to be asked is what we need. We aren't faced with a choice between guns and butter, but guns and bread.

In the fall of 1980, I visited half a dozen big Air Force bases, talking to people about missiles. I'm not a technically literate person and it took quite a while for me to grasp how some of these things work. An inertial guidance system, for example, or the MIRVing process by which a single missile can target ten or more sites on the ground with stunning accuracy. I came away from all of these conversations with the same impression: that the men I had talked to were able and conscientious, that there was no limit to what technology can be made to do, and that outside the gates is the world of the Miracle Mile, where everything is quick, slick, and cheap, and running downhill. In a missile everything is the best—the machined fittings, printed electronic circuitry, floating guidance systems, computerized fuel ignition, and so on. But in the world where we all live the subways are filthy, the cars are plastic and vinyl, nobody can afford to buy a house, the kids aren't learning anything in school, college tuition has just gone up twenty percent, Chrysler is tottering on the edge of bankruptcy, the steel industry needs special protection to survive, there are more people employed by McDonald's than by Ford. You can continue the list as well as I can.

We know what Reagan wants to do, and we pretty well know why. But tell me: is this really going to make us *stronger?*

10. HOW ACCURATE
IS ACCURATE?

One of the better-kept secrets of World War II was the fact that bombers had a hard time hitting anything—that is, anything *in particular*. The Norden bombsight was popularly believed to allow "surgical strikes" and "pinpoint bombing" but one man's pinpoint, as the Strategic Bombing Survey revealed after the war, was often another man's cow pasture. Bombs were dropped all over Europe, but rarely on target. A major U.S. daylight raid on the German ball-bearing plants in Schweinfurt in August, 1943, was typical. A total of 1122 high-explosive bombs weighing 395 tons was dropped by 376 bombers. The 8th Air Force later concluded there were 88 "direct hits"—that is, bombs which landed in the general plant area—and 55 actual strikes on factory buildings. The rest of the bombs landed somewhere, too, of course, and killed about 300 German civilians, including 26 children, and another 100 slave laborers from Poland and France. In the course of the raid about 60 U.S. bombers with their eight-man crews were shot down—roughly one for every bomb that landed on a factory building. The ball-bearing plant, while damaged, was soon back up to normal production.

The 8th Air Force and the British Bomber Command referred to this sort of thing as "strategic bombing," which they hoped would shorten the war. It did not. German air defenses forced the bombers to fly too high for truly accurate bombing, and the British, at least, decided early in the war to fly only at night. Freeman J. Dyson, the British-born physicist now at Princeton, worked on operational research during the war, and was often appalled at the poor results when he drew up bomb plots after the raids. In his memoirs, *Disturbing the Universe*, Dyson describes the reaction of one Bomber Command official to a preliminary bomb plot recording the results of a raid on Frankfurt. "Awfully few bombs inside the circle," the official said. "You'd better change that to a five-mile circle before it goes in."

Another Bomber Command study, conducted earlier in the war, examined the actual results of bombs dropped by pilots—about half of those taking part in the raid— who *claimed* to have hit the target. Impact photos showed that only one in four had actually dropped bombs within *five miles* of the target.

This inability to hit things accurately with bombs had several results. One was a high level of gratuitous killing and destruction. Hundreds of thousands of civilians were killed by the three million tons of Allied bombs dropped on Germany. Their deaths did not shorten the war by a day. Another result was a change in strategy, from "pinpoint" bombing of important factories, railroad marshaling yards, dry docks and so on, to "area bombing." Flying at night at high altitudes, the British switched targets to something they felt they could hit—cities. The new approach, never officially acknowledged, called for destroying the industrial suburbs where workers lived. But even putting it that way is a kind of euphemism. The target was simply people, on the theory that killing enough of them would crack civilian morale and perhaps spark the sort of popular revolution which ended the First World War. This was a failure too. On two occasions—Hamburg in July, 1943, and Dresden in February, 1945—firestorms were created which turned huge areas of the target cities into smoking wastelands, killing scores of thousands of people, but the effect on German war production was negligible. In the final stages of the war against Japan the Americans, too, finally abandoned the illusion of "pinpoint" bombing and adopted the British approach. Early in 1945 a huge 1000-plane raid generated a firestorm in Tokyo which leveled thousands of acres of housing and killed more people than either Hiroshima or Nagasaki. Cities we could hit, but cities weren't the enemy. Pain we could cause, but pain doesn't win wars.

It is accuracy which determines the efficacy of violence in war. In this regard battle and boxing have much in common. Boxers bob and weave and jab but they do not often land a solid punch. Even one or two, properly placed, can be enough to do the job. War is much the same. It is highly particular. Weapons make an opponent formidable, and it is weapons which must be destroyed. But weapons and the men who wield them are somewhere, and it is there a blow must be landed to be effective. Five miles away won't do. Down the street won't do. The blow must land on the exact spot where a soldier or a tank or a submarine *is*. In modern war the emphasis has been on volume of fire, not marksmanship, as a means of hitting an enemy. The machine gun, the artillery barrage, and carpet bombing are all ways of directing many lethal missiles to the general area where the enemy is. The law of averages is expected to do what aiming cannot. It takes tons of munitions to produce a single enemy casualty in this way, but production is what modern industrial states are best at. Nevertheless, the goal has always remained accuracy—a particular blow on a particular spot—and the recent development of precision-guided munitions threatens to transform war on the battlefield. The technology which raised volume of fire to nightmarish levels now allows us to really *hit* things.

With nuclear weapons, in spite of their great power, the importance of accuracy is equally acute. In the popular mind The Bomb is a weapon of Armageddon, a tool of apocalypse, an instrument of total destruction, a means to obliterate an enemy. But who is "the enemy"? Ordinary citizens in crowded cities, men and women like you and me, the victims—not the planners—of war? The first bomb was dropped on Hiroshima because a city was something we could hit. The day of the bombing Truman described the city as a military target, but it was nothing of the sort, as he doubtless knew. It was just a place so big you couldn't miss it, and so crowded with people the result was bound to be on an unprecedented scale of horror.

The plan worked. At any rate, the war ended shortly thereafter. Ever since, cities have been high on the target lists and their dwellers have lived unhappily with a kind of vision of the way the world will end. But it is important to recognize that cities did not become targets because that's where "the enemy" is, but simply because they are big enough to find at night and to hit. The American military—and very likely the Russians as well—were unhappy with this approach. They wanted to win wars, not murder half the globe. As soon as military planners on both sides began to get more accurate weapons, they aimed them at different targets, generally of a military nature. The most important military targets, of course, are weapons, and the most dangerous weapons are nuclear weapons.

This change has been a long time in coming. In the late 1940s and early 1950s the U.S. Air Force had little confidence in its ability to hit things. The B-47 bomber was thought to be doing fine if it dropped its bombs within 2500 feet of the target. With the advent of thermonuclear weapons this was close enough to destroy pretty much anything fixed on the ground, but of course the bombers took so long to arrive there was no chance of finding the enemy's bombers still on the ground. His most important weapons, therefore, could not be destroyed. Missiles were quicker, re-entering the atmosphere at better than 10,000 miles an hour, but the early warheads were so bulky, and the whole vehicle so technically crude, that the CEP of the first American ICBM—the Atlas—was "several miles," probably about five. CEP means "circular error probable" and refers to the radius, generally given in nautical miles, of a circle around a target within which half the missiles aimed at it will land. A CEP of 5 nm. means half the missiles will land within 5 miles of the target.

The earliest missiles stood up in the open and could be knocked over by a firm shock wave. Five miles was close enough. So the Americans, and later the Russians, put their missiles underground in silos, and then hardened the silos with steel and concrete. They made them very hard indeed. An ordinary brick house in the Georgian style, say, would be largely destroyed by an overpressure of 5 pounds per square inch, or 5 psi. No one knows just how hard modern missile silos are, and the military estimates are naturally classified, but the professional literature on these matters cites figures of 2000–4000 psi. Hardness to that degree means that a missile silo could be destroyed only by a direct hit—a warhead detonating sufficiently close by to put the silo inside the fireball (about a mile in diameter for a 1 megaton burst in the air), or inside the crater (about half a mile in diameter for a 1 megaton burst on the ground). This suggests that a missile intended to destroy a hardened missile silo would require a CEP of about 0.4 nm. for a 1 megaton warhead. There are many other factors which must be weighted in estimating the "probability of kill" (the PK) of a given warhead against a given target, but the most important of them by far is accuracy. That is also the factor which has generated the most argument during the last few years.

The argument, highly technical in its extended form, centers on a claim by a group of defense analysts in Washington that the Soviets now have missiles sufficiently accurate to serve as counter-force weapons—that is, to pose a threat to our weapons of fixed location (Minuteman silos, bombers on airfields, and nuclear submarines in port). The Soviet counter-force threat is cited as a principal argument for building the MX or some other, perhaps mobile, land-based system of *un-*fixed location, and for building counter-force (i.e., accurate) missiles of our own. A second group of defense analysts claims the first is crying wolf where the Soviets are concerned, and that the advent of counter-force weapons will destabilize the balance of terror by pushing both sides to fire first in a crisis, rather than run the risk of losing its weapons on the ground. In the literature this is referred to as the "use it or lose it syndrome." A further danger posed by a counter-force threat is the fact that the best defense against it would be a computer-controlled launch-on-warning system. This might "save" the threatened weapons (by using them) but it would make the world hostage to computer-error, which while it might be improbable, could never be impossible. Then, truly, the human race would have surrendered its fate to Fate.

The argument over counter-force accuracy centers on three points. The first is whether *any* missile can have a reliable CEP on the order of 0.1 to 0.3 nm. The Air Force, which periodically fires Minuteman III missiles from Vandenberg Air Force Base in California to Kwajalein Lagoon in the Southern Pacific, claims we are already within that range and that the MX will do even better. One Air Force officer told me a year ago that he and his colleagues routinely cite CEPs in terms of feet, and another said the second-generation MX, already being designed, will have a CEP of about 90 feet.

The second point of contention, pressed by the cautionary critics, concerns the question of bias—the known *tendency* of any missile to miss the target. Bias is a fixed quantity, a number like CEP, which represents the distance between the center of a cluster of impact points and the intended target, as established by actual test results. A missile with a CEP of 0.25 nm. might have a bias of 0.1 nm. According to the defense consultant Richard Garwin, an authority in these matters, *every* missile has a bias, and it has *never* been predicted in advance. A bias can have many causes—idiosyncracies of the hardware, gravitational anomalies along its flight path, severe weather conditions in the area of re-entry. American missile tests are mostly conducted from East to West across the Pacific. An attack on Russia would require firing over the North Pole. The cautionary critics argue that variations in bias make CEPs unreliable. The trouble with this argument is that ICBMs have been tested over a long period of time, and results show whatever they show. Military and technical men who have studied the results generally insist the missiles can really attain the accuracies claimed for them. Charles Draper, the Einstein of missile guidance who runs the laboratory named after him at MIT, recently published a letter in the *New York Times* in which he admitted the bias problem but said the point was whether it was "greater than the lethal radius of the warhead . . ." Back in the late 1940s, when missile-designers were still thinking in terms of 5 nm. CEPs, Draper predicted we would eventually get to 0.1 nm. No man has had more to do with making American missiles accurate, and he claims bias is not greater than the lethal radius. "There is indeed grave risk in using ballistic missiles," he concluded, "but that risk is not uncertainty of accuracy."

But the point of contention most difficult to settle involves the problems in coordinating the launch of many hundreds of missiles so that their warheads would land pretty much simultaneously on their targets, a *sine qua non* for a successful first strike. For one thing, many of the missiles would have to pass through the same "window" at the apogee of their trajectories in order to land on contiguous targets. Another problem is "fratricide"—the danger that warheads exploding on target will destroy others as they arrive nearby. A coordinated mass launch involves so many unknowns and imponderables that Jimmy Carter's Secretary of Defense, Harold Brown, once referred to it as "a cosmic throw of the dice." What ruling group, the cautionary critics ask, would risk the fate of its regime and country on something which has to work perfectly the first time?

But this shifts the whole discussion from a technical point to a debating point—from the question of accuracy to a question of Russian intent to prepare for a first-strike. From time to time, since 1945, the defense community in Washington has alarmed itself with claims that the Russians were close to achieving a genuine first-strike capability. The "bomber gap" of the early '50s and the "missile gap" of a few years later proved chimerical. The current episode of fear has not yet ended. But talk of first strikes has an unreal quality to it. With a handful of fanatic exceptions, not even the military believe the Russians are craftily preparing a surprise blow. The first-strike argument is in fact little more than a useful theoretical tool for comparing the characteristics of weapons. It is the technical point, the question of accuracy, which really matters.

It is our genius as a species to be able to find a way to do anything we can imagine. The truth of the matter is that missiles are accurate enough to serve as counter-force weapons. They can destroy anything on or reasonably near the surface of the earth, so long as we know where it is. The long history of technical improvement of inertial guidance systems has reduced CEPs from miles to fractions of miles to hundreds of feet. Further improvements in accuracy can be expected from terminal-guidance—that is, homing techniques—and from satellite navigational systems. The significance of accuracy is not that it clears the way for a first strike. The cautionary critics are right about that; a regime would have to be crazy to contemplate such a thing. But in the event of war it would be equally crazy to let alone what immediately threatens—weapons and the systems which control them. Accurate missiles prepare the ground for nuclear *war*—extended fighting for purely military objectives, a clash of weapons. No one doubts such a war would wreck the world. It is said that the towns in Germany are only two kilotons apart. But missile accuracy makes such a war possible and indeed forces the hand of military planners. If you *can* destroy enemy weapons, you *must*. This fact is now the driving force behind American nuclear weapons policy, the thing which explains what we are building and why we are building it.

II. CROSSING THE NUCLEAR THRESHOLD

The big things in history tend to start off in small ways. It's easy to miss them, or to read them wrong, or to point them out before they're really there. But departures have a seismic signature all their own, and the tremor was unmistakably underfoot in August of 1980, when a new strategic policy was announced by Secretary of Defense Harold Brown, a man who has spent his entire professional life designing nuclear weapons and deciding what to do with them. Brown insisted the policy was not new at all, but only an "evolutionary development" in American theories of how to keep the peace. This was just talk. In fact the world came full circle; a lot of new arguments finally lost out to an old argument. The great open questions of nuclear weapons—what to point them at, and why?—were finally answered by the world's military men, not the civilian strategists who had long sought paradoxical shelter in the prospect of Armageddon. The result is a return to Clausewitzean concepts of warfare, which identify the object of military operations as destruction of an enemy's military forces. This amounts to a silent crossing of what is now called the nuclear threshold, and its most important effect over time will be the absorption of nuclear weapons as one more item in the military inventory.

The new strategic policy, laid out in a document called Presidential Directive 59, comes in response to a decade of debate about Soviet military intentions, but its real cause is not a sudden revival of early Cold War fears of global ambition in Moscow. Specters are in the eye of the beholder. Some see them, and some don't. The real cause of PD 59, which calls for pointing American strategic weapons at Russian military targets, rather than industrial and population centers, is technical improvement of missile guidance systems, coupled with development of Multiple Independently-targetable Re-entry Vehicles, known as MIRVs. Accurate MIRVs have changed nuclear weapons from the hammer-like to the rapier-like—if anything with such pronounced side-effects (called "collateral damage" by the military) can be likened to a rapier. Argument about intentions is by its nature inconclusive; an intention is not a definite thing. The ultimate arbiter of military planning is what an enemy can do. Accurate MIRVs make it possible for missiles to destroy small, well-protected targets, which tend to be military in nature. The United States has 1000 missile silos dotted about the Great Plains which are small, well-protected targets of precisely this sort. Accurate Russian MIRVs which can destroy them have been a long time in coming, but they are here now and PD 59 is a form of recognition of that fact. With it we pass into a new era of nuclear history.

The horror of nuclear weapons was recognized from the beginning, but their military utility took longer to identify. The scale of their destructiveness was well-suited to large targets like cities, while the weapons themselves could be hidden or protected. This disparity between offensive capacity and defensive vulnerability—the ability to destroy, the inability to prevent one's own destruction—suggested a kind of permanent stand-off, a stable peace based on the "impossibility" of war with such catastrophic consequences. Robert S. McNamara, Secretary of Defense between 1961 and 1968, took this *de facto* stand-off, gave a name to the fear which sustained it—"mutually assured destruction"—and then saw to it that U.S. strategic weapons would be sufficiently invulnerable ("survivable") to threaten "unacceptable" damage to Russia in the event worse came to worst. He figured Moscow would consider the loss of a quarter of its people and half of its industry as unacceptable. Technical studies suggested that 400 one-megaton warheads could do the job. As a practical matter the United States deployed 1054 land-based missiles and 656 submarine launchers, a good deal more than enough to guarantee McNamara's unacceptable 25 and 50, but this did not alter McNamara's basic concept of a nuclear peace enforced by mutual Russian and American vulnerability to nuclear horror.

The McNamara doctrine had two great strengths as a strategic concept. The first was that it recognized, and made use of, the disparity between offense and defense. It turned vulnerability into a source of serenity, rather than fear. The second, which we can assume to be deeply rooted in the modern psyche, is the broad popular desire to believe that nuclear war is too terrible to happen. This is not limited to laymen. If anything it is taken even more firmly for granted by defense professionals who have been paying attention to the details. The guarantee of "mutually assured destruction" made war "crazy," so crazy that sober fear could be counted upon to override all the traditional proximate causes of war. The great appeal of MAD—to use the acronym coined by the civilian strategist Donald Brennan—was that it appeared to guarantee no more wars, or at least no more big ones.

After the First and Second World Wars, which all but wrecked Western civilization to no purpose, the promise of no more big wars probably reached about as deep into the human soul as it is possible for official words to go. If war was too terrible to happen, it wouldn't happen.

There is much which might be argued against a notion of "security" based on men's commonsensical reluctance to do something really stupid, but the argument which has finally closed the era of MAD is a military one. The bedrock of mutually assured destruction was the "survivability" of one's retaliatory forces. One side might destroy the other's cities, but not his missiles. McNamara ensured the survivability of American missiles by putting them in concrete-hardened underground silos and hiding them in submarines beneath the sea. This worked until the Russians developed new missiles like the SS-18, which can deliver ten separate MIRV warheads—each with an explosive power equal to more than a million tons of TNT —within a quarter of a nautical mile of the intended target. Where I live, that is less than the distance between the New York Public Library and Grand Central Station —roughly two crosstown city blocks. No hardened missile silo could survive a hit that close. This means that American Minuteman missiles are no longer "survivable." If we are to threaten Russia with assured destruction of the sort which makes wars too terrible to happen, we can't do it anymore with land-based missiles at a known location.

The opponents of the new strategy implicit in PD 59 argue that the Russian missiles aren't really all that accurate, and that our submarine-based missiles—not to mention our B-52 bombers, tactical weapons in Europe, bombs which might be delivered by carrier-based naval aircraft, etc. etc.—are more than enough to dissuade any prudent Russian government from attacking us. It is also argued, but somewhat more tepidly, that we can preserve our deterrent—that is, our power to retaliate crushingly —by switching to a policy of launch on warning. As soon as various technical surveillance systems detected a major Russian launch our own missiles would be fired automatically, thus escaping destruction on the ground. The fact that the decision would be in the hands of a computer, subject to sudden electronic twitches, makes this approach unattractive.

But in any event the arguments have now become moot. Military men and many civilian strategists have been brought to a state of quite agitated alarm by the prospect of a Russian capacity to destroy American land-based missiles in a surprise attack. Others may argue all they like that we've still got plenty of deterrent, and that the Russians will continue to be cowed by it. Others argued the Russians would never have enough missiles, accurate enough, to threaten Minuteman. They were wrong. The military will not be reassured by anything short of an ability to destroy their hard silos too. When the military is truly alarmed about something—not just faking it to beef up the budget—it is eventually going to get its way. The long argument about the U.S.-USSR strategic balance has finally focused down onto a purely military question—what their weapons can do to our weapons—and our response, embodied in PD 59, is a purely military one.

From one point of view the advent of military targeting for nuclear weapons is more shadow than substance, because targeting, as a practical matter, has always tended to concentrate on military and industrial sites chosen by the Pentagon. Even at the height of McNamara's tenure as Secretary of Defense, the assurance of 25 and 50 would have been the result of missiles dropped on military bases and industrial districts, rather than on population centers *per se*.

The changes implicit in PD 59 do not come from the choice of military targets, but from the primacy to be given Russian missiles and command centers, the direction of new weapons' development toward greater power and accuracy, and the commitment to a practical ability to fight a nuclear war one stage at a time, instead of jumping to the final holocaust or spasm-war stage right at the start. This is more than merely a shift in emphasis. If Hiroshima introduced the first era of nuclear weapons (that of the bomber-dropped bomb, with its threat of isolated acts of terror), and the advent of missiles *circa* 1961 marked the second era (with its threat of wholesale terror), then PD 59 marks the third era (with its full-scale return to Clausewitz, and the domestication of nuclear weapons as tools of war like any other). This does not necessarily increase the likelihood of war, but it will certainly affect the course and scale of war when it comes. At least four broad changes in the military situation are implicit in PD 59, although it is difficult to say which will have the severest practical results.

The first and most obvious is that military targeting is what nuclear strategists refer to as "destabilizing." In McNamara's formulation the peace was stable so long as neither side could do anything to protect itself. Fear of consequences would make men prudent. Military targeting is destabilizing because it suggests we can limit damage to ourselves by destroying their weapons with our weapons (or *vice versa*), and further that we can destroy all of their weapons (or at least their land-based missiles) with only part of our weapons (or *vice versa*). Of course, if we can hit their weapons at all—which PD 59 explicitly says we intend to be able to do—then we can hit them first, out of the blue. This will naturally heighten the tensions in a serious crisis, because both sides will grow jittery that the other side may decide to strike first for whatever marginal advantage is offered. If we could hit *all* their missiles—submarine-based missiles too—the situation would really be unstable. PD 59 doesn't make the situation completely unstable, just more unstable.

The American military and many civilian strategists have been arguing for years that the Russians have been building a first-strike capacity, whether or not they really intended to carry out such a strike. This remains in doubt. But they will now certainly adopt a military targeting policy of their own to match ours, if they have not done so already. It ought to be pointed out here that Russia depends much more heavily on its now-vulnerable land-based missiles than we do. PD 59 is bound to cause them very great concern, since it openly avows what we only suspected them of planning. Within a year or two the land-based missiles of both sides will be fully vulnerable to surprise attack. Is this the sort of thing the Russian or American military will contemplate with equanimity? Can launch on warning be far behind? The pressures for it will certainly be very great.

The second result of PD 59 will be more weapons. One convenience of the doctrine of mutual assured destruction was that it suggested the possibility of "enough"—enough destructive power to guarantee McNamara's 25 and 50, which, if 25 and 50 were truly "unacceptable," and were truly assured, would be enough to prevent a war, no matter how many weapons the other side might have. Military targeting does away with all such limits. We are never again going to have enough. For one thing, there are a great many potential military targets besides an enemy's missiles. More important is the fact that security of offensive capacity can be guaranteed only by the factor of MIRVs. If each Russian missile could destroy five American missiles, for example, we would have to have something more than five times as many to ensure some would always be left. But these could be MIRVed as well, so the Russians would need five times *that* many for the same reason we need five times as many as they. It's impossible to say just how far down this road we will go, but it's sobering to remember that an Air Force Chief of Staff in the 1960s strongly recommended to President Kennedy that the United States deploy 10,000 Minutemen, *ten times* the number McNamara eventually decided would be enough. More weapons will be more expensive, of course, but the really troubling aspect of more is that there will be more to go off when war comes.

A third broad implication of PD 59 is that a major nuclear war would not necessarily end in a matter of hours or days, as once seemed likely to be the case. One aspect of the new policy calls for provision of a "secure strategic reserve," by which is meant a stock of weapons buried so deep, or hidden so well, the Russians cannot possibly destroy them. Doubtless the Russians will match this capacity too. It is not hard to imagine a war in its third or fourth day, with both nations all but totally ruined hulks, while some small residual force on both sides continues to haul out weapons from the secure strategic reserve and fire them at the enemy. I once stopped by a field in Egypt to watch a man plowing with two oxen and a wooden plow. His plow did not even have a metal tip. While I watched, two Egyptian air force jet fighters screamed by overhead; each one cost millions of dollars and I thought of the terrible distance between the world of the pilot and the world of the plowman, and wondered a bit at that aspect of the human fate which always guarantees the millions will go for better planes rather than better plows. Survivors may live to see such a disparity in our own country.

In some ways the secure strategic reserve is the most frightening aspect of PD 59. At the very least it implies no more international arms agreements, since monitoring a reserve would require inspection on the ground, which the Russians have been adamant in refusing to allow. But we have not been very successful in negotiating arms agreements anyway, so the practical implications of PD 59 in that regard are probably not important. The prolongation of nuclear war is something else again. In the past it was assumed such a war would be terrible but soon over. PD 59 ensures the agony will be prolonged. The survivors' natural sorrow for what has been lost will be all but overwhelmed by fear of its repetition.

These implications of PD 59 all make it a significant document. It would be helpful if we might read it in full. But the fourth implication, already suggested, is the most important of all. Pointing nuclear weapons at military targets, and thereby emphasizing their nature as weapons, marks the beginning of a sea-change in the psychology of Russian-American confrontation, a gradual acceptance of the possibility of war. Military and civilian leaders will of course go on saying their purpose is to prevent war, but there is a vast difference between saying that war is inherently too terrible to happen, and that we are too strong and alert to be challenged successfully. I never had much confidence in the long-term efficacy of the first approach, but at least it encouraged a sober frame of mind. The military approach borrows all the language of deterrence, while attempting to balance forces in the manner of the great European powers before 1914. They also felt peace was to be found through strength, and that war would never begin so long as all sides knew what they were up against.

For the moment nothing seems changed; we are still prepared for Armageddon, both psychologically and militarily. But within a very few years things will be quite different. We shall deploy different kinds of weapons in different kinds of ways. We shall probably begin a civil defense program (since that is the clearest evidence of willingness to fight a limited nuclear war, which Brown said is the point we were trying to get across). We will protect our weapons in ways which preclude arms agreements. We will be subject to heightened tension whenever the United States and Russia edge towards a serious crisis, as we do every two or three years. Exactly when the inherent instability of such a situation will assert itself is impossible to say, but it ought to be clear that the better "prepared" we are, the more we have got to fight a war *with*, the worse it will be.

From the day of Hiroshima forward it has been apparent that nuclear weapons meant trouble for humanity. It might even be argued that no one has felt truly light-hearted since. But thirty-five years is a long time to keep something in mind; young men have grown old and died since 1945, while the problem has grown steadily more complicated and intractable as technical progress has made the weapons more versatile. It is the weapons, in fact, which have been leading the way, not we the weapons. No short essay can possibly do the subject justice. It takes long study just to gain familiarity with the words, and after that it requires a sustained effort of the moral imagination to keep hold of what the words mean. What

I have written here is the barest outline of the argument which led to PD 59, and of the consequences we may expect from it. These necessarily lie in the future, which we can see only dimly. Discussions of the problem posed by nuclear weapons in the immediate postwar period all recognized the extreme danger, even the likelihood, we would do ourselves severe damage—they saw the future clearly enough for that, just as we can—but at the same time they were groping, inexact, and often wide of the mark when it came to details. They were especially wrong when trying to answer any question beginning with when. The same is likely to be the case now. PD 59 is not a step in the direction of safety or peace. But like the other large things in history, precisely where it's taking us will all be more apparent in retrospect.

12. WHAT IS WAR?

For the last thirty years of his life, Karl von Clausewitz (1780–1831), the great Prussian military writer, tried to complete the sentence, "War is . . ." The many attempts all add something to our knowledge of war, at once the most common and the least understood of human enterprises. But Clausewitz was never quite satisfied with the results.

In his major work, *Vom Krieg* (On War)—never finished and published only after his death—he tried to reduce war to its essence again and again. "War is an act of violence to compel our opponent to fulfill our will," he wrote on the first page of his book. Later he amended his definition to read, "War is an act of violence pushed to its utmost bounds." Even his best-known formula comes in many variations, all making the same point in slightly different words. His final choice is the one most often quoted. It was discovered after his death in a note apparently written in 1827. There he said, "War is only a continuation of State Policy by other means."

The austerity of this dictum has earned Clausewitz a reputation as the supreme rationalist of military thinkers. But in fact he was both romantic and passionate; in other circumstances he might have been a poet or scholar. It was history—the revolutionary upheaval which began in

1789 and ended at Waterloo in 1815—that posed war as the central question of Clausewitz's life. He was introduced to war at the siege of Mainz in the summer of 1793, a thirteen-year-old cadet in a Prussian infantry regiment. On June 18 Prussian cannon opened fire on a trapped French revolutionary army. The city's wooden houses were soon in flames, food and water were in short supply, horribly wounded soldiers were left to die without care, clouds of smoke hung over the city as the awful cannonade went on for nearly five weeks.

The siege of Mainz was a brutal battle; perhaps five thousand French soldiers, as well as three thousand Prussians, died before the surrender on July 22. But Clausewitz, like any other boy in a uniform on the periphery of the worst horrors, was swept up by the thrill of the thing. "I stayed while Mainz was being burned to the ground in the fire we had started," he wrote later. "I added my childish shout to the triumphant cheers of the soldiers."

War was Clausewitz's life, as it was Europe's, for the next twenty-three years. He fought at the battle of Auerstadt in October 1806, where the Prussian army was shattered by Napoleon; in the terrible Russian campaigns of 1812, where the ravages of winter were as deadly as the rifle and cannon; and in the final battles of Napoleon's eclipse, ending at Waterloo. But the real theme of Clausewitz's life was thinking about war, not fighting. His romantic streak led him to write to his wife often of the beauty of death in battle, but his daily work focused on the reform of the Prussian army with his mentor and friend, Gerhard von Scharnhorst, and on saving the nation from the timidity of its king, Friedrich Wilhelm III, who was more interested in details of uniform than tactics, and always chose the wrong moment to fight.

The key to Clausewitz's thinking was the fact that it

grew out of a profound national crisis. During the years of Napoleon's dominance in Europe, the Prussia of Frederick the Great was reduced to the status of minor power, neglected and scorned. At times it seemed the kingdom might even be carved up and swallowed entirely by its more powerful neighbors. Clausewitz neither glorified war nor sentimentalized its horrors. He did not think of it as a tragedy to be avoided—a kind of natural calamity —but as the only possible solution to a genuinely desperate problem.

"Let us not hear of generals who conquer without bloodshed," he wrote. "If a bloody slaughter is a horrible sight, then that is ground for paying more respect to war, but not for making the sword we bear blunter by degrees of humanity, until someone steps in with one that is sharp, and cuts off the arm from our body."

This realism gives Clausewitz's thinking about war a business-like cast. He concerned himself with nothing but the political significance of the outcome, and it is here that he departs most dramatically from the traditional military mind. "The politician should fall silent the moment that mobilization begins," said the elder Helmuth von Moltke, chief of the Prussian General Staff, later in the century. It was this attitude that Clausewitz fought throughout his career. For him the objects of war and diplomacy were identical. Sometimes one method was appropriate, sometimes the other. Above all was the importance of a sense of proportion: military operations must be in scale with political goals, and risk commensurate with gain. One did not go to war lightly, nor seek more than was reasonable from victory, nor fight on senselessly when defeat was already clear. Like Clemenceau after him, Clausewitz thought war too important to be left to generals who care for nothing but who wins.

For him the important questions were why wars start, and how they end. Military "victory" merely prepared the ground for acceptable terms of peace.

Hence his dictum, "War is only a continuation of State Policy by other means." Clausewitz tried to remove the mystery from war, to see it as the doing of men rather than the working of fate. This seems an entirely sensible approach to the problem. It offers a way to tame the chaos, give point to the suffering, and even limit the damage. But does it really describe what war *is*? Consider for a moment the background of Clausewitz's life—war upon war for two and a half decades, involving some of the greatest battles of history in which scores of thousands often died in a single day. In Napoleon's Russian campaign of 1812 alone, only a few thousand returned from a French expeditionary force of half a million. The rest were captured, died in battle, drowned crossing the River Berezina, starved, froze. Moscow was not the only city burned in those years. It all seems mild enough compared to World War II, perhaps, but Europe was exhausted for decades thereafter. The victors longed only to go back to 1789, to forget the intervening horrors. It is here that Clausewitz's dictum reveals its limits. If the victors wanted nothing from their victory but the way things had been, what were the Napoleonic wars *about*?

Throughout those years Clausewitz concerned himself with the fate of Prussia, threatened in 1792 and then crushed and in effect occupied after the military disasters of Jena and Auerstadt in 1806. First the army failed the king, and then the king failed the army. With the aid of Clausewitz and others, Scharnhorst rebuilt the Prussian army, but the timid king would not risk war again, despite abundant provocation. Napoleon was a master not only of battle, but of studied national insult. In 1812 he humbled Prussia yet again by forcing Friedrich Wilhelm to join his war against Russia and even to provide a 20,000-man corps. This was more than Clausewitz could bear. He was intoxicated with patriotic ardor; his letters of the time reveal a positive longing to die rather than witness further national humiliations. The king might submit, but not Clausewitz. He resigned his commission and left to fight with Russia, the last continental power still willing to resist Napoleon.

But if we join Clausewitz in explaining war as what properly follows the sort of provocation Napoleon visited upon Prussia, how do we explain this sort of provocation? War was not Prussia's doing alone, but Napoleon's as well. If we are to explain what war *is*, then we must account for both factors in the equation. It is not enough to say that war is sometimes necessary. The fact of its necessity is part of its nature.

At this point the mystery is reintroduced. The Napoleonic era was one of military cataclysms which, like the cataclysms of 1939–1945, are for convenience blamed on the overweening ambition, the charismatic power to lead, and the human recklessness of individual men—Napoleon in the first instance, Hitler in the second. We have no difficulty explaining why others chose to resist. Napoleon and Hitler crammed war down their neighbors' throats. It is the wars themselves, seen as a single dark whole, emerging out of nowhere, that leave us mystified when we try to say what war *is*. Looked at in this light William Tecumseh Sherman's definition—"War is hell" —serves better than Clausewitz's. Indeed it is hard not to conclude that Clausewitz was not defining war at all, but trying to give it a rationale, to find some thread of reason in the chaos, to rescue us from despair in the face of something so blindly destructive.

This aspect of war did not escape Clausewitz. "It is quite possible," he wrote, "for such a state of feeling to exist between two states that a very trifling political motive for war may produce an effect quite disproportionate —in fact a perfect explosion." It was "perfect explosions" that Clausewitz tried to prevent with his emphasis on policy. Clausewitz did not tell us what war *is,* but rather urged us to approach it in a mood of utmost sobriety.

The limits of Clausewitz's view are a matter of more than academic interest, for the simple reason we cannot hope to avoid war indefinitely if we don't know what it is. Ensuring that we do avoid it is, of course, the central question of our time. The destructive capacity of nations now is vastly greater than it was in Clausewitz's day. Modern delivery systems for nuclear warheads—missiles, manned aircraft, and submarines—are so constructed and controlled they might go on "fighting" after their sponsors were all dead. "Violence pushed to its utmost bounds" is now beyond the capacity of society to bear.

Both the United States and the Soviet Union appear to understand this fact. In 1958 Khrushchev told the Yugoslav ambassador to Moscow, "The Soviet Union will continue to fight stubbornly for peace, which we have especial need of for the next fifteen or twenty years. After that no one will be able to go to war even if he wants to." Khrushchev meant that war would be too terrible to make sense, and he was right. For both great powers the preservation of peace is thought to rest on a single point: the certainty of "unacceptable" consequences in the event of war. Guaranteeing that certainty is at the heart of every debate on weapons systems, and the effort has so far been a successful one. But it has not made us feel safe. We know war is irrational, but fear it anyway, without quite being able to put our finger on the ultimate source of danger. At the heart of this fear, I think, is the suspicion that war is not really policy—a rational enterprise—in the sense Clausewitz intended, but something darker and less predictable, something which happens to us without reason or purpose.

No statesman seems willing to concede this possibility, and it's not hard to see why. If the sheer horror of nuclear weapons is not sufficient guarantee they will never be used, then we are even closer to the edge than we generally allow ourselves to think. It is probably inevitable that we assume the choice for war is always ours.

But history seems to be telling us something different, and nowhere more clearly than in the years 1914–1918. Where do we find a thread of reason in that calamity? The war began and continued without rational motive, a collision of great armies which bled Europe until Germany collapsed in agony. We have lived too long with the results to believe the blind commitment to victory made sense. That, truly, was "an act of violence pushed to its utmost bounds."

Clausewitz did not shrink from this side of war. Few have written with such scorn of those who would include pity among its principles. But Clausewitz could not bear to think of war as violence alone. I think it must have been the poetic streak in his character which led him to insist that war has another face. When he came to sum up a lifetime of war and thinking about war, his objectivity failed him. He did not find reason at the heart of war, but only hoped to put it there.

13. BACK TO THE
COLD WAR

There is only one crucial question facing the modern world, and I guess we all know what it is. It's odd to go back and read *The Guns of August* and think of the time and effort the Great Powers of Europe put into finding ways to speed up mobilization. A day or two might make all the difference then, when my father was a young man. Now he's an old man and it's hard to imagine a major war in which mobilization would matter at all. It wouldn't take long to fire off all the rockets, and after that little would be left but the odd plane or two over the Arctic, on its way to deliver a final, vindictive bomb.

No one would win such a war. No one in his right mind could want such a war, and yet such a war could easily happen. Some people even think it will certainly happen. Major General George J. Keegan, Jr., who retired as chief of Air Force intelligence in January, 1977, thought the Russians expect such a war, are planning for such a war, and may even think they could win such a war. If General Keegan is right we are obviously in bad trouble, but how are we to determine if he is right?

Occasionally a news story comes along which reporters can only grope about in like men in a darkened room, and this is one of those stories. It involves the most fundamental issues of war and peace and it is the subject of the fiercest sort of controversy, but most of the evidence on both sides is secret, the participants are mostly keeping mum, and journalists must feel about for truth with little more than instinct to guide them.

The question of Soviet intentions, of course, is an old one. It is hard to know if the American conflict with Russia is more like Britain's with France in 1816, or Rome's with Carthage. God knows there has been no want of Catos. I once asked a friend and colleague of Allen Dulles in Berne during World War II when it was that Dulles began to shift his concern from Germany to Russia. "Stalingrad," she said.

When the CIA was established in 1947 its major target was Russia, and since the early 1950s its most important piece of paper every year—the document which absorbed the most time and money and aroused the bitterest dissension—has been the "Annual Survey of Soviet Intentions and Capabilities." The first few "Surveys" were about 25 pages long. By the mid-'50s they were up to 100 pages and now they're as much as 400 pages divided into several volumes filled with charts and graphs, facts and figures, touching on just about every facet of Soviet military might and strategic purpose.

The early "Surveys" were short partly because the CIA did not have much information to go on. Most of it came from agents in Europe run by the CIA itself, the British SIS and the German intelligence agency headed by Reinhard Gehlen, who had been in charge of German military intelligence on the Eastern Front during the war. There was a good deal of uncertainty about Russian military matters because agents found it hard to operate in the "denied areas" of Eastern Europe and Russia, with their huge and efficient security services.

Now that has all changed. The introduction of U-2

BACK TO THE COLD WAR

flights in 1956 and of spy satellites a few years later, in
addition to the enormous volume of electronic intelligence—radio traffic, radar signals and the like—collected
by the National Security Agency, has allowed the CIA to
establish with great accuracy just what the Russians have
by way of planes and tanks, submarine pens and hardened
missile sites.

That leaves the question of Soviet intentions. As intelligence officers never tire of pointing out, you can't photograph a "forward plan" from the sky. With the exception
of Oleg Penkovskiy for a year or so ending in the fall of
1962, the CIA has never had a high-level spy in the Krem-
lin, which means that Soviet intentions have always been
very largely a matter of conjecture. Since we simply don't
know what Soviet leaders are saying in the Politburo, we
must deduce it from what we do know. This leaves plenty
of room for argument, to say the least.

"After the Czech coup in 1948," DeForrest van Slyck,
an early member of the CIA's Board of National Estimates (BNE), told me in 1976, "it wasn't a matter of
whether they were going to attack, it was just when.
Would it come in 1950 or 1951? Or would they wait until
1955?

"For years the military would come in with these in-
flated estimates of Soviet military capabilities and intentions. They were *all* aimed at the budget. The Air Force
would argue they've got the capability of building such-
and-such a number of bombers, so they're *going* to build
them, so three or four years from now they *will* have 800
bombers."

Since the United States had both nuclear weapons and
air bases well within reach of Russia the military had to
posit some credible Russian threat to the mainland U.S.
Otherwise a war would be brutally one-sided and a poor

bet from the Russian point of view, with the implication the Russians would hardly be *planning* such a war. The American military's solution to this dilemma was ingenious: one-way bombing. Russian bombers could not reach U.S. targets and return, but they could make one-way suicide runs. For years one-way bombing was the sole, even faintly plausible Russian threat to the U.S. the military could come up with.

"The imagination that has gone into the Russians," Van Slyck said. "They never built up their bomber force at all to amount to anything. They jumped right to the missiles, but the military never stopped making the worst case. It's this mania to keep ahead. It never seems to occur to these military men that what the Russians do is out of apprehension. If they could have heard those Air Force generals, my God!"

At that time, and until the system was changed by William Colby, National Intelligence Estimates (NIEs) were argued over by the BNE and then later by the United States Intelligence Board (USIB) chaired by the Directors of Central Intelligence. Early NIEs were sometimes the result of so many compromises and qualifications that they were all but indecipherable, but under General Walter Bedell Smith the estimating process was tightened up. If one of the USIB members, the Air Force or the Navy, say, could not be convinced of the CIA's view, it was forced to put its dissenting view in a footnote. Since footnotes had a way of coming back to haunt the dissenters, they were relatively rare.

But even so the process of estimating Soviet intentions demanded a degree of compromise. No one could know for certain, after all, what the Russians were actually planning. "Our answer," said one BNE chairman at the time, "is to say nothing is going to happen in the foreseeable future, and say it in the most alarming way possible."

The intelligence battles over Soviet intentions are as fierce now as they were in the early days of the Cold War. Back in August, 1969, Richard Helms, then Director of Central Intelligence and chairman of USIB, deleted a paragraph on Soviet intentions from an NIE on Russian strategic forces after an indirect but unmistakable order from the Secretary of Defense, Melvin Laird. The point at issue was of central importance, the CIA estimators saw no reason to change their view, and the matter was clearly within CIA's jurisdiction, but Laird had his own ideas on the subject, and Laird won. It's worth quoting the paragraph in full to give an idea what the fighting is about.

We believe that the Soviets recognize the enormous difficulties of any attempt to achieve strategic superiority of such order as to significantly alter the strategic balance. Consequently, we consider it highly unlikely that they will attempt within the period of this estimate to achieve a first-strike capability, i.e., a capability to launch a surprise attack against the U.S. with assurance that the USSR would not itself receive damage it would regard as unacceptable. For one thing the Soviets would almost certainly conclude that the cost of such an undertaking along with all their other military commitments would be prohibitive. More important, they almost certainly would consider it impossible to develop and deploy the combination of offensive and defensive forces necessary to counter successfully the various elements of U.S. strategic attack forces. Finally, even if such a project were economically and technically feasible the Soviets almost certainly would calculate that the U.S. would detect and match or overmatch their efforts.

It ought to be clear that the view expressed here is a fundamental one which goes to the heart of the whole question of peace and war. In the CIA's view Russia was not trying to achieve military superiority over the United States, was not planning a pre-emptive war against the United States, had a healthy respect for U.S. power, and by implication understood that it could not bully the world, but must reach an accommodation with the U.S.

Laird's reason for suppressing this paragraph was not necessarily a belief in the Russian bogey out to conquer the world, but a lot of other pessimists in the intelligence community do believe in the bogey. One of the gloomiest was General Keegan, whose dissent was so fierce in 1974 that he was called to the White House to argue his case. Partly as a result of his repeated warnings the CIA's estimating process was altered in 1976 to include an outside team of seven Soviet and defense experts who operated something in the manner of devil's advocates, challenging the CIA's team of Soviet experts led by Howard Stoertz. The document which came from their sometimes acrimonious deliberations (to judge from the name-calling which has surfaced since) was described by the CIA as a "more somber" view of Soviet intentions.

It is not clear just what "more somber" meant, but it apparently included a guess that Russia spends 11 to 13 percent of her gross national product on arms, rather than the 6 percent or so estimated by the CIA a year earlier; that Russia has been consistently increasing spending on arms while the United States has been reducing it and that Russia enjoys a clear superiority in many types of weaponry, and is aggressively pursuing superiority in others. No one seemed to be saying that Russia was building a first-strike capability or was planning a kind of nuclear Pearl Harbor. Foreseen instead was a possible preponderance of Russian arms of the very sort the United States enjoyed in the Caribbean at the time of the Cuban missile crisis. An independent group of pessimists ranging from Saul Bellow to Maxwell Taylor and William Colby, calling themselves the Committee on the Present Danger, said a new balance of power may soon exist in which "we should face, one after another, bitter choices between war and acquiescence under pressure."

The change in the CIA's estimating process and the broad outlines of the argument have emerged rapidly since the *Boston Globe* first broke the A team/B team story in December 1976. General Keegan became something of an instant celebrity, after years of quiet labor in the intelligence vineyard. There has been a degree of anonymous boasting and complaint by the two teams' experts. George Bush, then director of the CIA, and Leo Cherne of the Board of Intelligence Oversight both deplored leaks about the new Soviet estimate, and President Carter was placed on constructive notice that he faced a strong arms lobby which was fundamentally out of sympathy with détente.

But the controversy also raised a stark question which journalists have been visibly reluctant to state baldly, and which they clearly do not know how to resolve: Either the pessimists were right, and increased Russian military spending is evidence of Russian ambition, or the CIA's estimating process, after decades of independence and rough honesty, had finally been politicized.

A lot of skeptics think the CIA's estimates have been political for years, but I don't think that was the case, or at least not entirely the case. During the war in Vietnam, for example, there was terrific pressure on the CIA to find some benefit in the bombing program, but you can read the Pentagon Papers from beginning to end without ever finding an estimate which said the bombing was going to "work," in the sense that Lyndon Johnson, Walt Rostow and the Air Force wanted it to work. At the same time, typically, the CIA never said it was *not* going to work either, while conceding, with a bow to the Air Force, that it was doing a lot of damage, was "hurting" the North, was making Hanoi's supply efforts more "costly," etc. The compromise on that issue was a lot like the compromise on the question of Soviet intentions back in the early 1950s, when the CIA said nothing was going to happen, but said it in the most alarming way possible.

That is a long way from the "more somber" view of Russian intentions in recent NIEs. How, then, are journalists to judge their accuracy, much less their honesty, when they are blocked from all the detailed intelligence data which are the basis of the estimate, insofar as they have a basis; and when participants in the debate will give only cryptic or garbled accounts of what it's all about?

My own instincts tell me that the pessimists are wrong, that the Russians are genuinely committed to détente, not as a cover while they secretly prepare for war, but as the best way of avoiding war. Instinct tells me that the Russians must have learned the lessons of the twentieth century, having suffered from them so much already. Instinct tells me you have to be slightly crazy to think the Russians would be willing to lose everything above ground for the pleasure of doing even worse to us. And it is something like instinct that leads me to believe we are watching a tentative replay of the 1950s, an effort by the pessimists, perhaps only half-deliberate, to reestablish the Cold War consensus that once insulated the defense and intelligence communities so effectively from scrutiny. But I can't say I know these things to be true.

14. A QUESTION OF INTENTIONS

The day after the sixty-third anniversary of the Bolshevik Revolution, celebrated in the traditional way with a huge military parade through Red Square in Moscow, there appeared an equally traditional photograph on the front pages of the world's newspapers of the leaders of the Soviet Union. In the center was Leonid Brezhnev, a heavy man made even bulkier by a greatcoat. His features are coarse and full—great round cheeks, large nose, dark and bushy eyebrows. He is said to be a sick man and his swollen, apoplectic aspect, as if his tie and shirt collar were cutting off his windpipe, is said to be the result of his illness. But he did not look sick otherwise. His expression was one of confident content, and perhaps a trace of pride. His eyes were half-closed. It may have been the wind, or weariness after standing so long, or simple inwardness, like the dreams of a man who has been carried back inside himself by a piece of music. It was impossible to look at Brezhnev's picture—a kind of facial echo of the goosestepping Russian army units, the tanks which roared through Red Square at twenty or thirty miles an hour—and not wonder: what is this man thinking?

But wondering is as far as we can go. No one in the West really knows what any of the Russian leaders are thinking. Of course every man remains something of a mystery to himself and others, but the culture of Russian Communism seems to have suppressed every note of the personal. Western political leaders leave a broad trail behind them of speeches, interviews, profiles in newspapers and magazines, the remarks of friends, the reminiscences of old political allies and enemies, the transcripts of press conferences. Even Richard Nixon, perhaps the most enigmatic political personality in American history, has left a rich paper record. If we include the tapes of his private conversations and phone calls, his may be the richest archive in history. It may not be easy to say what animated him, ultimately, but there is certainly plenty of evidence to work with.

Nothing of that kind can be found to help explain what Brezhnev is up to. I say nothing. Doubtless that is too absolute a word. I have read that Brezhnev is—or used to be—a chain-smoker of cigarettes, and that he is a sucker for fancy cars. Perhaps his love of ostentation in cars can explain that trace note of satisfaction about the mouth as he watched the cream of the Red Army march by. Perhaps not. It certainly isn't much to go on in trying to plumb the plans of one of the world's two great powers, especially when he and it have spent something over a trillion dollars and fifteen years building a military machine which is arguably the world's biggest. Something more must be going on there than a love of parades.

But what? Americans trying to figure it out have come up with two quite distinct explanations of Russian behavior since the Second World War. One says the Russians are moved primarily by fear, self-doubt, and anxiety. Twice in this century Russia has been invaded by the West. Each time perhaps twenty million Russians were killed before the violence ended. If man learns by experience, the theory goes, then the Russians have learned caution from theirs. Twice burned, thrice shy.

Two other factors are said to contribute to Russian fear of the world. One is a long history of being treated as not quite civilized, a crude and brutal race beneath the notice of Western Europe. The French-speaking Russian aristocracy was taken as something of a joke in the casinos and watering spots of Germany and Austria-Hungary. The imperial pretensions of Czars rested on a clumsy serf army beaten in the Crimea, by the Japanese in 1905, by the Germans on the Eastern Front in World War I. The diffidence and self-doubt derived from such mighty failures have been compounded, according to this theory, by the isolation of the Bolshevik regime which replaced the Czars. Inept Western intervention which prolonged a bloody civil war got things off to a bad start and the unrelenting hostility of Fascist regimes between the wars only made matters worse. Thus Russian national history, Communist ideology which defines Capitalism as a mortal enemy, and the horrors of World War II, followed by a kind of worldwide anti-Communist crusade led by the United States in the 1940s and 1950s, have all combined to maintain a climate of paranoia in Moscow. The result has been a single-minded drive for security based on military might pure and simple.

The second theory of Russian behavior, currently returning to favor in Washington, treats the first as so much eyewash. Russian history is important, certainly, but what is that history? Relentless imperial expansion to the East into China, to the South into Central Asia, to the West into the Baltic states, Poland, and the Balkans. The Bolsheviks simply glossed this drive with a justifying veneer of Marxism-Leninism and went right on pushing wherever the way was clear, into Mongolia, into Finland and Poland in 1939–40, into Central Europe and the Balkans during the Second World War, and most recently into Afghanistan on a beeline for the Persian Gulf. Russian intentions are no mystery, the second theory says. Communist theory holds there can be no permanent peace between Socialism and Capitalism, and the Russians have been building an army to back up their ambitions, which are global. When they were weak they were cautious. Now they are strong and are beginning to flex their military muscles.

These two interpretations of Soviet behavior, far from being academic exercises, are in effect the party lines of two great circles of like-minded men who have been pushing each other out of power in Washington since 1945. A cynic might argue it doesn't really make much difference who's in office since the military results are roughly the same—an ever larger American military establishment with a decisive edge in strategic weapons which is only now coming into question. The reason it matters which theory is correct is that a reasonable response to an aggressive and expansionist Russia—the drawing of a firm line, with power to back it up—is the very thing most likely to inflame the fears of a Russia which is anxious, self-doubting and easily spooked. The reverse is just as true: a low-key, soothing, unthreatening approach to Moscow would tend to encourage expansionist dreams. If the Russians themselves were more forthcoming—if they wrote more, answered more questions, submitted to more interviews, routinely published their memoirs, cultivated the note of personal authenticity—it might not be so difficult to determine which is the real Russia, if either. But this they will not do. Their memoirs tend to the proper and the wooden, and their theoretical work is opaque with Marxist-Leninist pieties. The result is an argument without end.

One reason the argument receives so much attention is that it provides a model for trying to predict Russian behavior—referred to in the intelligence business as "intentions." Intelligence people like to say you can't use a satellite to photograph a forward plan. This is intended as an argument for traditional agent-running. The trouble is you can't photograph an *important* forward plan with an agent either; they are simply too hard to recruit, and Russian security is too efficient. Satellites are awesomely inclusive when it comes to Soviet "capabilities"— what it's got in the way of military hardware—but their intentions are hidden from us. We have got to figure them out, and that is not at all easy to do.

In the first place an intention is not a thing. An army is large and hard to hide. A tank gives off heat and leaves tracks. Nothing looks like a submarine except a submarine. An airfield is long enough for big bombers, or it isn't. But an intention is the gossamer stuff of the mind, a potential of the will, an assertion of hope. In geopolitical terms it is what a group of ambitious men are willing to commit to paper about matters with the capacity to wreck both career and country. In the first instance, then, an intention is a document which may be locked up in a well-guarded room.

But American intelligence officials never (or very rarely) obtain the critical documents of the Soviet government. They must infer what the Russians are up to by what they do. In the second instance, then, an intention is a pattern of behavior. At this point we run head-on into the two basic theories of Soviet behavior, since what they do is not really in contention. Officials in the Carter Administration never denied the Russian shipbuilding or

ICBM upgrading programs (although they tended not to see them quite so soon as their opponents); what they resisted was the pessimistic view that the Russians were deliberately building all this hardware in order to push us around.

It's not hard to see why they resisted. The consequences, if true, are bound to be unpleasant. If Russia, for whatever combination of reasons—ideological, economic, the sheer exuberance of men who find they can have their way—is embarked upon a course of advantage-grabbing backed up by missile-rattling, then the result, soon or late, will be war. The new generation did not really win the argument; it is too problematic for that. They have uncovered no dramatic new facts. Russian military building has been extraordinarily energetic, but that might be explained just as well by the depth of their insecurity as by the reach of their appetite. Russia has been preparing to fight—not just to endure—a nuclear war, but that would be a perfectly rational response on the part of men terrified one is coming. What Russia does and says are consistent with either of the two theories, and most people probably make a choice between them on the basis of temperament. As a nation we respond to what they have got, and a few years down the line they will doubtless respond to what we have got.

It may be that nations do not really have intentions, but only a history and a character. It may be that Russians become fearful, anxious, and insecure whenever we toe up to them pugnaciously, trying to curb dangerous ambitions before they get out of hand. It may be that they grow confident, overweening, and greedy whenever they sense the pressure easing during those periods when we try to reassure them before panic takes hold. It may be that nations have distinctive temperaments—predispositions towards kinds of behavior—and that they don't choose how to deal with their neighbors, any more than the lion chooses a taste for meat. If that's the case, we're in the dark. But then we're in the dark anyway. The Russians do not betray themselves as a nation. Brezhnev does not betray himself as a man. The half-closed eyes and enigmatic smile are not evidence enough to tell us what he is thinking. He may be patiently laying the groundwork for the triumph of world Communism in the by-and-by, or just dreaming of a warm drink, the taste of a cigarette, the struggles of his youth, the sheer damned difficulty of getting anything *done*, the smiling men all checking his skin color in the morning, and waiting to take over.

15. THE MORAL FALLACY

Be England what she will,
With all her faults she is my country still.

"The Farewell"
CHARLES CHURCHILL (1731–1764)

One day in the summer of 1981—it was a drizzly Saturday morning—I drove up to Montpelier, Vermont, with a friend, Virgil B., to join a group of several hundred marchers completing a three-day walk from one small Vermont town, Washington, to another, Moscow. The marchers' goal was an American-Soviet nuclear weapons freeze. Since both countries are engaged in a rapid strategic arms buildup, the proposal of a freeze, seemingly a cautious one, is actually quite radical. It is the heart of a common program adopted by a wide range of peace groups who met in Washington in the fall of 1980.

Virgil and I arrived just as the marchers were setting out on the penultimate leg of their walk to Waterbury, a distance of 3.2 miles. Another friend, Alan R., had been on the march with two of his sons, ages seven and nine, since the beginning. As we walked along in the drizzle under umbrellas, herded well to the side of the road by marshals from the American Friends Service Committee,

Alan told us his adventures of the previous two days. Several things had struck him. Whenever the group came to a likely body of water, for example, a group of young women immediately stripped and went swimming naked without apparent embarrassment. A tall, lean, good-looking man of forty or so asked him—not once, but several times—if he thought he could spot the government agents who were taking pictures and writing down names. Since this fellow admitted to a background in security work, Alan began to wonder if *he* was the agent in question.

Alan also said he now understood why protesters all looked like unkempt hippies. After a day or two living in the open you tended to be festooned with gear—canteen over a shoulder, things stuck in your belt, a headband to keep the sweat out of your eyes, odd buttons pinned here and there, walking stick, etc., etc. But the thing which struck him most was the sharp division between the veterans who started out on the first day and the groups which joined later. The earlier groups tended toward a faint disapproval of the later, as if they didn't quite grasp what it was all about, or exhibit the proper demeanor, or share the same degree of commitment. In time, as still tardier arrivals appeared on the scene, the distinctions faded away.

In Waterbury, about noon, the marchers all filed into a local church where they were to be addressed by a Russian arms control expert, Yuri Kapralov, who had been sent by the Soviet embassy in Washington. Originally he had been scheduled to speak in Moscow at the end of the walk, but at the last moment the State Department declared Moscow off-limits for Russians. The marchers were all damp from the drizzle and the church was crowded, hot, and steamy. Kapralov was a youngish man with black horn-rimmed glasses and a good command of English despite a pronounced accent. He clearly knew the language and issues of strategic arms debate in Washington, but his talk skirted most of the details and centered on Russia's desire for arms agreements, its equanimity with the idea of a freeze, and its vivid memory of the horrors of World War II. After his talk he answered questions from the audience. Most of the questions were friendly, although a few offered Kapralov an opportunity to defend or justify the total absence of independent peace groups in Russia—an opportunity he, for the most part gracefully, declined.

Before it was over Virgil was visibly squirming in his seat. I asked him what he thought. "Slick propaganda," he said. "He just turned the audience around his finger. It made me sick." Questions had been piling up in his mind: What about Sakharov? What about Afghanistan? What would happen to Poland if we had no theater nuclear forces in Europe? Kapralov's every friendly word—skirting all the difficult questions—just made Virgil madder and madder. He had been going through a period of intense melancholy, common to people when they first begin to think hard about nuclear weapons. He had been seeing things with new eyes—the cities which might be destroyed, the green earth which might be poisoned, his own children who were hostage in a global confrontation. But when Kapralov stuck to those very things, the vagaries of peace, it made Virgil mad.

I once spent the better part of a year trying to figure out why the Arabs and the Israelis could not make peace. My technique was to read history, paying close attention to the details. I started with Theodor Herzl and the beginnings of the Zionist movement, when Palestine was often described as a kind of unpeopled wasteland. I spent a lot of time on the 1920s and '30s, when Britain began to think better of the Balfour Declaration. The infamous White Paper, limiting Jewish immigration at the very moment of Hitler's rise, and the intrigues of the Grand Mufti of Jerusalem, seemed especially significant. I followed the postwar diplomatic maneuvering which led to British withdrawal and UN support for an independent Israel. I did not neglect the massacre at Deir Yassin or the bombing of the King David Hotel. And so on and so forth through all the wars, the rise of the Palestinians, the UN resolutions and the various peace initiatives, down to the present day. Finally I went to the Middle East and spent six weeks talking to people—not famous people but not quite ordinary people either, passionate partisans for both sides.

From this exercise I learned one useful thing—nobody is right. There is no single thread of justice. You can't add up all the violence, the honest and dishonest acts, the atrocities and heroic sacrifices. The history of the place is not a history of wrongs and rights—something you can judge—but a history of two entities in collision. Each defends itself. One question overrides all the others: who gets to call Palestine his own? As outsiders we can understand what is happening there, but we can't figure out who is right.

Q : *What about Poland, Hungary, Czechoslovakia?*
A : What about Guatemala, Cuba, Chile, Indonesia, Iran?
Q : *What about Afghanistan?*
A : What about Vietnam?
Q : *What about Hafizullah Amin?*
A : What about Ngo Dinh Diem?

Q: *What about Masaryk?*
A: What about Lumumba?
Q: *What about Sakharov?*
A: What about Martin Luther King?
Q: *What about the kulaks?*
A: What about the Negroes?
Q: *What about the purges, Gulag, Lubyanka, Siberia?*
A: What about Dresden, Hamburg, Hiroshima, free-fire zones, Agent Orange?
Q: *What about the SS-20?*
A: What about Pershing, GLCMs, SLCMs, ALCMs?
Q: *What about fifty thousand tanks in Eastern Europe?*
A: What about the neutron bomb?
Q: *What about world revolution and the triumph of Communism?*
A: What about "the last best hope of mankind"?
Q: *What about Khrushchev, "We will bury you"?*
A: What about Sen. Richard Russell, "If we have to start over again from Adam, I want to be sure he's an American"?

This sort of thing will get us nowhere. When it is used to explain the Cold War, it is fundamentally dishonest. Political acts have moral aspects, and it is a sign of civilization to try to keep them in mind, but justice is not the motor of history. We do not oppose and arm against the Russians because they have been found guilty in a formal proceeding conducted with strict respect for the rules of evidence. Enmity between nations is more mysterious than that. At the start of *The Peloponnesian War* Thucydides cites but rejects the popular explanation of the war, based on various crimes of Sparta and Athens. Some of these were crimes all right—especially the Athenian massacre of a recalcitrant ally—but Thucydides claims the real cause was Sparta's fear of growing Athenian power.

It is the same with Russia and America. Throughout World War II in Washington and London there was a kind of muttering undertone of hostility toward Russia, a State Department–Whitehall alarm, deep in the bowels of bureaucracy, that Stalin was no less a threat than Hitler. General Leslie Groves, the director of the Manhattan Project, once told a colleague that within weeks of taking on the job he was convinced that "Russia was our enemy and . . . the project was conducted on that basis." Allen Dulles, chief of the OSS office in Berne, Switzerland, told a friend he began to switch the focus of his concern from Germany to Russia after the battle of Stalingrad, when it became clear Hitler could no longer win. General George Patton wanted to drive right on to Russia in 1945. This was not the inevitable friction of allies but something much deeper, a Western fear of Russian size, appetite, and "backwardness"—the city-man's fear of a sullen, barbarian horde—which goes back deep into the nineteenth century. It is not anger at what Russia has done which explains the Cold War from the Western point of view, but fear of what Russia is.

The Soviet Union has indeed done many terrible things. So have we all. Someone once said that history is the record of crimes. But war is not an instrument of judgment. It may settle things from time to time but it does not discriminate. Bigger battalions are simply bigger battalions. The history of the Cold War does not add up to a compelling conclusion that one side is right and the other wrong. It is simpler than that. We are on our side and they are on theirs.

One afternoon in 1975, in a farmhouse not far from the Sea of Galilee, I spent a couple of hours listening to a roomful of Israelis try to explain their country's failure to make peace with the Arabs. In large part they blamed themselves—they had been too confident after the Six Day War in 1967, they couldn't make up their minds about the West Bank, they were too unbending with the Palestinians, they relied too heavily on arms. It was an extraordinary performance in the act of self-criticism, the more striking after two weeks in Beirut listening to Palestinians. The Palestinians all seemed to have read the same book. They disagreed with each other about the proper form of socialism to be established in Palestine after the liberation, but on every other point they were unanimous. It appeared they were totally free of all blame in the conflict, going right back to the 1880s. It was a Jewish invasion from the beginning, the land must be returned to its rightful owners, and there was no more to be said about it.

This was purely a difference in character. It said nothing about who was on which side. The Israelis I listened to had all been in the army, had all fought in one or two wars, had all been wounded. All continued to serve 60–90 days a year on active duty, and all were ready to fight again. They judged their country, but would not abandon her. I thought about this on the drive back from Waterbury, Vermont, after listening to Yuri Kapralov skate over the differences between us and them. It had been a practiced performance all right, but what else was he to do? They're on their side, and we're on ours. Some of the things they have done stick in the craw, but what of it? Doubtless they feel the same way, and what of that? Both pale beside what we have prepared to do to each other, in the name of defense.

16. THE PRINCIPLES
OF ABOLITION

In 1945, even before the Trinity test proved an atomic bomb could be made to work, a sudden wave of concern or alarm swept the laboratories where the new weapon had been fashioned. Military authorities had done their best to keep everybody in the dark, to isolate Oak Ridge, the Met Lab in Chicago, and Los Alamos, and to treat all general discussion of the bomb as a violation of security. Scientists didn't like it, but for the most part went along. But early in 1945, when the magnitude and the imminence of the bomb became apparent, the scientists—in a single, spontaneous, almost convulsive awakening—suddenly grasped the thing whole: the bomb was big enough to wreck our civilization, there was no defense, any determined nation could build one, an arms race could result in stockpiles of thousands, something had to be done. Churchill and Truman were slow to understand the bomb was not simply bigger. For the Pentagon, then as later, a weapon was a weapon. It was the scientists alone, throughout 1945, who understood what had happened, and what must be done.

Robert Bacher, at Los Alamos, was one of them. He had been working on the bomb since 1943. In August, 1945, he personally checked out the core of a bomb intended for a third Japanese city, while a military team waited outside, motor running, to carry it to the airport for the first leg of its flight to the Pacific. At the last minute orders arrived not to send the core. Instead it remained at Los Alamos. The American stockpile of nuclear weapons may be said to have begun at that moment. In the following months Bacher was active with the Association of Los Alamos Scientists—known without irony as ALAS—in what came to be called the scientists' movement. It was clear to Bacher what had to be done: the world had ten years at the outside to find a way to control nuclear weapons, or some awful calamity would eventually follow. The ten years passed, nothing was achieved, the calamity is still pending. Now a professor emeritus at the California Institute of Technology and a veteran of many government commissions, Bacher hopes he was wrong, that the world's failure to reach agreement does not really mean disaster. But the hope is not robust. "It's a miracle we've got this far," he said recently. Perhaps it was a miracle. Perhaps we've been given time for a second effort. Who can say? One thing is clear: attempts to control nuclear weapons in the last thirty-six years have failed. There are thousands now, and thousands more on the way. Nothing stands in the way of the disaster Bacher and so many others foresaw but fear, and the hope that fear is enough. The scientists who were active in 1945, asked for a gambler's guess of our chances now, fall into two rough groups. Some think we may squeak through. Others think not. It seems to be a question of temperament. Whatever they think, naturally all are hopeful. Talking to these scientists, or to others in what is called the national security community, one hears a great deal about hope. It is hope naked, hope pure, hope unalloyed with anything hard enough to point to as an actual reason. At this point in our history, it seems clear, optimism must be blind. We have built thousands of nuclear warheads, and we hope they won't be used.

Is this the best we can do?

One should not be too quick to answer. It may very well be the best. The history of efforts to establish varying degrees of international control of nuclear weapons—beginning with the ambitious and clear-sighted Acheson-Lilienthal plan of 1946—is dense with the serious work of able men. William Foster, Gerard Smith, Paul Warnke, Henry Kissinger, and Cyrus Vance, as well as many others both in and out of government, in this country and elsewhere, have done their best to fashion useful and enduring agreements and to explain the importance of the undertaking. Arms control is not a subject which has been neglected in print or in fact. But the history of these efforts is a history of failure, for the most part, while the history of the arms-builders records one triumph after another.

One might isolate any number of reasons for the failures of those who think there are too many weapons in the world, not too few. A major one is the tendency of any plan for controlling, limiting, or reducing arms to invert itself, to shift its focus from limiting weapons to an argument that X are enough. Thus arms negotiators and defense planners are in the same line of work; they attack the problem from opposite ends, but meet in the middle. In this perpetual debate at the official level all concede we need arms, including nuclear arms. Some say we need a great many, others say not so many. Naturally the president, who must decide, prefers to err on the side of safety. The result, since 1945, has been a slow, losing, rear-guard action by the arms limiters, and the building of a great many strategic weapons—not so many, perhaps, as the military would have liked, but more than enough to break the back of our civilization, when used.

This pattern is not reason for abandoning arms negotiations, but for something else—the building of a constituency which might take a different approach. The prospects for a new movement of this sort are dim at the moment. What might be the occasion for a spontaneous arousal on the necessary scale, short of a major war? This I cannot answer. But if such a movement came into being —a genuinely abolitionist movement, prepared to forgo nuclear weapons entirely, to work for *none*—on what basic principles might it build an argument? How might it justify—not only to the world's military and political leaders, but more importantly to itself—a claim that nuclear weapons are too dangerous and too wanton to possess in any number at all? It seems to me there are eight basic principles on which an abolitionist movement might found itself.

1. *It can happen.* Nuclear weapons do not make war impossible; they only ensure it will be terrible. The theory of deterrence is that war is an act of aggrandizement, and that nothing can prevent it but fear of the consequences. History suggests that war is something else—a characteristic and habitual form of human behavior, a thing men do—sometimes for one reason, sometimes for another. If we do not know the root causes of war how can we hope to prevent it—*forever?*

2. *All victims are equal.* How are we to choose between human beings, and say that the death of one somehow matters more than the death of another? War happens to both sides; it is the whole loss which diminishes mankind and is cause for sadness—not just the loss on our side. Very few of the dead had anything to do with starting it;

war simply came and took their lives away. In the sort of war where millions die the balance of the millions is immaterial. All the millions were innocent. Any serious attempt to save them must attempt to save all of them. Attempts to save our side only are simply military measures under a different name.

3. *Nothing can be gained or preserved commensurate with the loss.* War on a global scale cannot be said to be about anything. Nations have their differences, but it is impossible to conceive of one large enough or important enough to require the wrecking of the world. Such a war would simply happen. The issues involved at the outset would be overwhelmed by the war itself. Nothing the United States or the Soviet Union could do to each other in a non-military way could ever equal what they can do to each other in a military way. In the past it might have been said that war was about who wins. Now it is about what survives.

4. *Weapons threaten; they don't defend.* As a practical matter one can't protect oneself by threatening others. Threats elicit threats. There are distinctively defensive measures a nation might take, but building strategic weapons is not one of them. Thirty-five years of trying to guarantee our safety with strategic weapons has made us about as unsafe as any nation in history; it is the same for the Russians. This ability to injure each other has become the deepest source of conflict between the United States and the Soviet Union; it is the bedrock of defense policy. But defense is a misnomer; what we buy, for the most part, are not things which defend, but things which threaten.

5. *There is no military solution.* Weapons have not made us safe; more weapons cannot be expected to do any better. Attempts to gain or hold an advantage in weapons

have been the motor of the arms race, and have only increased our common danger. The fifteen thousand strategic warheads possessed by the U.S. and the U.S.S.R. threaten our civilization. The twenty-five thousand we are expected to have by 1985 may threaten human life in this hemisphere. Eventually we may acquire weapons enough to threaten all human life on the planet. This is not something either of us wants to do, and it is not something either of us would risk if it weren't for the peculiar context of pride and will which forms the background of an arms race. It is the weapons which threaten us, not the political differences. The problem isn't too few weapons, but too many. We need to get rid them, not build more. But insofar as the military sees weapons (theirs) as a problem, it insists that weapons (ours) are the solution.

6. *There are no villains.* The problem is not rapacious monopoly capitalism or militant Communism. Such claims are only a convenience. The scale of the present arms race is unprecedented, but otherwise it's the common stuff of history. Our reason for it is the common one too. The strategic weapons possessed by both sides threaten their mutual annihilation; why are we doing such a terrible thing? The easiest answer—the one that leaves us out—is villainous intent on their part, some great ambition we must resist. Thus our own military efforts can be seen as the solution to a problem. There is a problem all right, but it isn't the iniquity of the other side; it is our characteristic response to the fact of sides. The students of war have got hundreds to study; their causes come in dozens of varieties. Clearly men are ready to go to war for this reason or that reason or no reason; the reasons are only a kind of veneer. They describe without truly explaining the war. There is a corollary to

the no-villains principle: if the other side isn't the problem, then we aren't the problem either. It is our common nature which explains our behavior. Understanding war is not a polemical but a spiritual exercise. To free ourselves of war we must understand and transform ourselves, no easy task.

7. *We can never forget how to build nuclear weapons.* The threat they pose is now a permanent part of the human situation. Even if complete abolition of nuclear weapons were achieved, no system of international inspection or control, however extensive, could prevent their renewed manufacture in the event of a big general war. Starting from scratch in August, 1942, the United States built its first nuclear device in less than three years. Next time the job would go quicker. Thus the danger posed by nuclear weapons is inseparable from the danger posed by war itself. The weapons reflect a dangerous part of our nature, not the only one by any means. We shall be struggling with it, one way or another, for as long as we are here to struggle. Arms control is a step in the right direction, but it is not enough.

8. *We do not have to submit.* The pattern since 1945 is clear; it is one of preparation for war. Our chances of altogether escaping this war are fragile, but the prospect of failure is no reason for submission. Why wait till war proves the point? The political and military establishments of the world do not really like living under the threat of annihilation any better than we do; they simply fail to see an alternative. Thus an attempt to free ourselves of war and the fear of war may be seen as a struggle toward the light—to see the danger as a common one, to grasp our own role in the process as well as our opponent's, to comprehend that the violence of modern war is out of scale with whatever it may be said to be about,

and finally to understand there is no way to threaten others without endangering ourselves in return. A move in this direction, away from war, must be personal before it can be political. It is worth undertaking for its own sake, whatever the results. We need no one's permission to begin.

17. THE WAY OUT
IS FORWARD

When Herodotus visited Egypt in the fifth century B.C. he found a decadent society, exhausted by time and the troubles of history, going through ancient motions by rote. Things were done as they had always been done, but woodenly, with frequent shortcuts. The origins of things had been forgotten, and even their meaning was dim. Formal learning was confined to a priestly class which guarded it jealously—so jealously, in fact, that the guardians themselves had lost their command of the ancient sciences. The great achievements of early Egyptian mathematicians—geometry, an estimate of the Great Year deducted from the procession of the equinoxes, even rudimentary forms of algebra—had so decayed they had to be reinvented or discovered by later thinkers, the Greeks among them. Or so I have read. Perhaps it isn't really true. Perhaps men can't forget things once they have been truly learned.

Like the Egyptians, the Americans have made an attempt to guard certain forms of scientific knowledge. When Howard Morland attempted to publish the "secret" of the H-bomb in *The Progressive* a few years ago, the government went to court to stop him. Morland did not know the full "secret." He had managed to figure out only a version of it, a notion of it, a suggestion of it.

Morland had never worked for the government, had never signed a secrecy oath, was not even a scientist. The government argued that none of that mattered. Under the Atomic Energy Act of 1946 not just privileged knowledge, but the ideas themselves, the very principles of nature involved in bomb technology were "born secret."

This was a very broad claim. In the event it could not be maintained. Another bomb buff who had figured out elements of the "secret" published his own version while Morland was still under injunction and the government dropped its case. But in a truer sense the battle had been lost years before. The principles of nuclear physics had become the common possession of mankind. The Russians, the British, the French, and the Chinese had all figured out how to make thermonuclear weapons on their own. According to a Los Alamos scientist I talked to last spring, Carson Mark, it is a small jump from fission weapons to fusion weapons, and the main barrier to the building of fission weapons is industrial, not scientific. Bomb design is easy; the production of fissionable material is an immense undertaking. Despite the government's claims, Morland did not reveal the "secret"; he only demonstrated that it was already widely known.

This fact tells us something important. We cannot go back. We cannot forget how to make nuclear weapons. We must live with the knowledge from now on. It took me a long time to grasp this principle, and I suspect others find a similar difficulty. We speak of "getting rid" of the bomb as if they might all be disassembled, the fissionable material buried in a salt dome, production facilities at Rocky Flats and Pantex turned into bird preserves, the technicians all sent out to teach or design toasters, the planes and missiles re-armed with conventional weapons, and the world returned to the *status quo ante*—say, 1939.

This would be unusual, but not unprecedented. Japan, for two centuries, gave up gunpowder and returned to the samurai sword. Why can't we—leaving aside for the moment the reluctance to do so of the White House, the Congress, and the Pentagon—give up the bomb?

In theory, at least, this is something we might do, and it is certainly something we ought to do. But it is important to understand what such an act of renunciation would achieve, and what it would not. At the moment the United States and the Soviet Union have about fifteen thousand strategic nuclear warheads pointed at each other, at least a third of which could be delivered in thirty minutes by missile. The rest could all be fired on the opening day of a war. The result, of course, would be catastrophic; we need not dwell on that. If we got rid of all those warheads, and the others in Europe as well, we would free ourselves of two things—the knowledge, which has been sinking into the human mind since 1945 like a stone into the sea, that any day might be our last; and the danger, in the event of war, that the firing of nuclear weapons might rapidly escalate in a panicky spasm of fear that it was now or never.

Clearly, international agreements which might free us of these two things would be a mighty achievement. There is no reason whatever to expect we shall get them, but they would be a marked improvement over the present situation, when the talk in Washington is all of more and better. But such agreements could not really free us of the threat of nuclear war. When the Manhattan Project got under way in August, 1942, the men who ran it had no clear idea how a bomb might be designed, and had never been able to manufacture even a gram of fissionable material. Kilograms were required. Nevertheless, the first bomb was detonated in July, 1945, just three years later.

Soon we could produce roughly a bomb a week. If Germany had held out another six months it might have been obliterated. How long would it take to build nuclear weapons now, starting from scratch? A few weeks? It is the knowledge which takes time to acquire, not the building of hardware. We know how to build bombs. We shall *always* know. We cannot go back.

The military offers another solution to the problem posed by nuclear weapons—standing still. Not quite still, of course; we must go on developing new warheads and delivery systems as technology allows. But so long as we are dangerously armed, and cannot be disarmed, and potential enemies know it, then war is extremely unlikely. This is the theory of deterrence. It explains why we can dare to have weapons we can't dare to use. In Washington the primary source of anxiety, which always runs high, is that the threat posed by our nuclear arms will come undone—that a defense might be found (generally considered to be remote), or that the other side will develop a capacity to disarm us in a surprise attack (generally thought to be around the corner). Of fear of war itself— the resort to arms as the outcome of a political crisis which cannot be resolved diplomatically—I have never found the least trace.

A couple of weeks ago I met an Air Force officer whose current assignment is tactical intelligence, which he does not like. He'd rather fly. This wasn't an interview, but a chance meeting. I'd known him in California in 1957 when he was ten or twelve. But we got to talking about defense policy and the Soviet threat and where Reagan would finally decide to put the MX, and I took the opportunity to ask him the question I try to ask everybody I run across in the defense community: how is it all going to turn out? We're thirty-five years into the age of nuclear weapons, more and better all the time, no sign of Soviet-American amity, what will happen?

"Nothing will happen," he said.

Nothing?

Nothing. We will just go on as we are, matching developments in the technology of weapons delivery, indefinitely. This is an all but universal view in Washington. Military officers, civilian think-tank strategists, National Security Council staffers, even arms negotiators all share it. Nothing will happen. We won't get rid of nuclear weapons, we won't settle our differences, we won't go to war. We will just go on as we are.

There are two difficulties with the theory of deterrence and the permanent stand-off. One is the rule that in history nothing never happens. We have had no big war since 1945, but the arms race has been far from stable. A great deal has happened. Weapons have grown steadily more accurate and versatile. The Buck Rogers push-button warfare feared in 1945 is approaching reality and the Reagan administration's renewed emphasis on command, control, communications, and intelligence (in effect, the wiring) will make centrally controlled nuclear warfare a genuine possibility. New technology—in the use of laser and charged-particle beams, in anti-submarine warfare, in depressed trajectory missiles—threatens the safety of the weapons on which deterrence depends. The very scale and capacity of weaponry has become a source of tension and conflict.

The second difficulty with deterrence theory is that it depends on a notion of war as a rational act of aggrandizement, something which can be prevented by fear of the consequences. This explains some wars—World War II, perhaps—but not others, and certainly not the First World War, which was also preceded by a long period of arms innovation, military buildup, international rivalry, and recurrent crises. When hostilities began in 1914 it was for largely technical military reasons having to do with the scale and rapidity of mobilization. There are many ways hostilities between the United States and the Soviet Union might begin, but very few ways they might end without recourse to nuclear weapons. In both Washington and Moscow, in fact, it is assumed that war means nuclear war, if not on the opening day, then shortly thereafter. Fear of the consequences—the existence of a deterrent—may ensure we won't embark on war deliberately, for gain, but it cannot guarantee war won't happen to us. For these reasons it seems to me that deterrence is only a stopgap, not a solution. We depend on it because we have not had the imagination to think of anything else. It may work sometimes, but we have no reason to think it will always work. We can't stand still.

The only way out is forward. By this I mean we have got to find some way of freeing ourselves from the danger of war itself, the one thing which is generally accepted as being impossible. Perhaps it is. But we have not got much choice. Nuclear weapons have brought something new into the world—a threat posed by arms so vast it undermines the last claims of war as a rational means of defense. This requires some new arrangement of the affairs of nations—a statement deliberately vague because I can't quite see what it is to be. Attempts to write a global constitution do not seem to get very far, and all seem to require a kind of policing force which sounds very much like an army. Fear of other people's armies is what defines the situation as it is right now. What we need is not a new army, but some way to be independent, to be different, even to be hostile, without recourse to arms.

The only route forward I can see is through arms

negotiations, but negotiations with a somewhat different emphasis. Limiting the numbers of weapons, or the development of new ones, is useful and helpful. It reduces the amount of hardware which might be available on the first day. But even more important, agreement—on arms or any other substantial matter of mutual interest—establishes a working climate of trust and cooperation. Negotiating focuses the attention of national leaders on what arms can do, since no ruler would surrender his authority to decide such matters. It allows nations to decide security questions on an ad hoc basis, one at a time, in the light of the moment. It reminds military men that peace is their goal, or at least requires them to say so in public. It encourages people to think security depends on agreements, not on threats of violence. It channels debate toward the language of justice, equity, and fairness. It tends to narrow differences, since even failures to agree generally do not fail by much. It serves as a model of a different sort of world, in which contracts would dominate. But perhaps most important of all, negotiations provide hope of a way out. The hope may be farfetched or illusory, but it's better than dreaming of simpler times, or standing still waiting for nothing to happen forever.

18. ARTIFACTS OF
THE RECENT PAST

A couple of summers ago, at an auction in Vermont, I saw a 1940 Indian motorcycle. It had been painted red. The seat was the sort they call a bicycle seat—triangular in shape with a generous cupping curve in the rear supported by two large springs. The feel of the seat was deep and liquid. Behind the seat were commodious leather saddlebags with chrome buckles, and in the righthand pocket was the original owner's manual. I don't know enough about motorcycles to tell you much about this particular model. I heard somebody say it had been built for the U.S. Army but was discontinued after the first thousand. Originally its color had been olive drab. It was a long, low, heavy, fat-tired machine, and I lingered around it, for reasons I can't easily explain, the better part of two hours. So did a number of other men. They stood there arms folded, admiring the solid curve of the front fender, the headlight on a swivel mount, the brass fuel pump. The men told motorcycle stories or World War II stories or just talked numbers—engine size, tire pressure, the price it might bring, the year Indian started in business, the year Indian went out of business. A rumor went around that a buyer for Robert Redford—or maybe it was Steve McQueen—had come a thousand miles just to bid on this machine. Nobody doubted it. I've forgotten

137

what it went for, but it was a good deal—as much as a new car with a lot of extras. I certainly didn't have that kind of money for a motorcycle I might ride twice a year and neither did any of the other men, but I don't think any of us thought the buyer a fool. We understood him perfectly. The true value of that Indian motorcycle—so miraculously preserved—could not be measured in dollars.

There is something curious about the charged talismanic significance of objects of recent origin. Age has little to do with it. It is not at all the sort of thing you might feel in a museum. Greek bronzes can stop you in your tracks and elicit a kind of cathedral mood, but there's a formal quality to the encounter. One is on one's good behavior. Perhaps this is the result of the typical museum setting—especially in this country where Greek bronzes are reverently displayed in rooms of immaculate white, dramatically lit from above. Naturally, with such an unmistakable nudge from the authorities, one speaks in whispers.

But that isn't the only difference between the truly ancient and the barely antique. The treasures from the tomb of King Tutankhamun are enough to put anyone into a thoughtful mood. In the national museum in Cairo, where I saw them in 1975, they were badly lit, crowded into display cases, erratically labeled, in no comprehensible order. At the Metropolitan Museum in New York the cues of lighting and setting could hardly have been more emphatic; the viewer was grabbed by the lapels and given a good talking to. It didn't really make much difference. The gold masks and jewelry and painted boxes looked pretty much the same in both places: breathtakingly old, fragile, and alien. Both times I remember thinking: this is our last chance to see so deeply into the past. Now these things have been found, they'll soon be lost, dispersed, and destroyed for good. You can't entrust things to men. They'd survived in the tomb since 1325 B.C. Can anyone in this world imagine the national museum in Cairo, or the Met in New York, will last 3200 years? Finding those objects, and putting them on display, is our way of destroying them.

A museum is a way of reminding us that all things pass. The objects precious enough to display there are a kind of proof how utterly dead and gone is the world which created them. The distance between us and them is very great; a museum reminds us that soon there will be no bridge at all, hardly more than the memory of a memory. These are interesting emotions and are one reason we have museums and visit them once a year, when it's raining on Saturday and the kids are restless. But looking at a Greek bronze, or a suit of French armor of the twelfth century, or even a Pre-Raphaelite painting is not at all like looking at a 1940 Indian motorcycle. No one personally misses Periclean Athens, but 1940—that was ours.

Not long after the auction a friend and his wife came for drinks and we got to talking about comic books. It turned out my friend and I had liked many of the same titles, especially the EC line which flourished for three or four years—the very briefest of Golden Ages—between 1950 and 1953 or '54: *Two-Fisted Tales, Weird Science, Tales from the Crypt,* and so on. The names and styles of the artists are still vivid in my mind, people like John Severin, who did the best Indians—I mean American Indians—in the history of comics; and Wally Wood, who did the best interiors of space-ships; and Harvey Kurtzman, a man of many-faceted genius (he practically invented *Mad,* among other things; the first *Mad,* the great *Mad*) and an artist of formidable power. Kurtzman did a number of stories about the Korean War—one called "if," for example, about a GI fatally wounded by a stray mortar round. In that story was all the blind meaningless chance of war. Another was about a house built by a Korean family, destroyed at the end by a single artillery shell. In that story was all the blind meaningless waste of war. Kurtzman may have been the greatest of them all, the perfect marriage of style and substance.

My friend remembered many of these artists and stories too. We are hardly alone in this. The collecting of comics is a robust industry, with trade magazines (called "fanzines") and annual conventions. The complete *Two-Fisted Tales,* for example, has been republished in four large volumes on heavy stock, $65 for the boxed set. It is not at all uncommon for the originals to bring $25 or $30 a copy, and the last time I checked, the price of the first issue of *Action* (the original home of Superman, the appeal of whom escapes me; but to each his own) was around $1,000.

My friend and I tried to find an explanation for the appeal of these artifacts. All sorts of answers jumped to mind. For one thing, of course, they were good of their kind. They reminded us of our childhood. They were completely outside the official culture crammed into us at school. They were bright and sensational. They are no longer published. Their survival is a kind of miraculous accident, considering the treatment they got and the paper they were printed on. They were ours. And so on and so forth.

But none of these explanations touched the heart of their appeal, the thing they share in common with all the other residue of their time—the baseball cards, Coca-Cola trays, World War II "loose lips sink ships" posters, movie stills, 45 rpm records, bomber jackets, Flexible Flyer sleds, table radios in wood cabinets, "I Like Ike" buttons, Mickey Spillane paperbacks, toy soldiers, Donald Duck watches, Lionel trains, old copies of *Fortune* filled with Packard and Cadillac ads, Stanley wood planes, wicker porch chairs, Prince Edward tobacco tins, gooseneck desk lamps. If you've ever been to a flea market you'll know what I mean. People wander slowly from stand to stand, solemnly fingering the artifacts of the recent past. A great poet might write a great elegy on this subject. In the nineteenth century the recent past did not exert such a tug on the emotions. That was a time of confidence that things were getting better. Everybody wanted the latest. The old was synonymous with the worn-out, the useless, the outmoded. The people of that time were great chuckers-out. Or so I imagine. It's different now. Things are moving quickly. Mere decades are as distinct as geologic ages. In a flea market it's all still there. You could pick your year and, given a little time and money, rebuild the vanished era down to the smallest detail—1940, perfectly preserved.

Things speak unmistakably of their time. Some time ago a friend and I, returning to the city from the country, passed an old Army & Navy store alongside the highway. Behind the one-story cinderblock building was a bomber. Olive drab tarpaulins covered the two engines and the cockpit. Neither one of us had ever seen such a plane before, outside of the movies, and we stopped to ask what it was. The wife of the owner told us it was a B-25 Mitchell bomber of the sort Doolittle used in his raid on Tokyo only a few months after Pearl Harbor. After the raid the planes had to be ditched in China or Southeast Asia, I forget where. They couldn't carry enough fuel for a round trip.

We went out back and walked around the plane. The

tires were flat, there were holes in the wing, we could see inside the fuselage through a missing door. I was about eighteen months old when Doolittle made his raid. My friend hadn't even been born yet. All the same, the B-25 Mitchell bomber is a relic of our past. Back then there was a strict limit to the range of a bomber. It didn't last long, and now the bombers can circle the globe.

You can fake a painting, perhaps, but you can't fake a plane, or a ship, or an old car. They are unmistakably of their time—something we have outlived. Things that are past are ours. In a sense they are safe, as we were too— then—had we but known it. Perhaps that is the source of their magic. When an old car passes down the street, everybody turns his head. There goes his childhood, which can no longer be disturbed.

Recently I came across an old photograph dated unmistakably by a car. It looked like a Chevrolet of 1937 or '38. It is parked in front of a small white frame building with a large sign on it, and an immensity of sky behind it. In large letters the sign reads: "LOS ALAMOS PROJECT MAIN GATE." Below it in smaller letters is the legend: "Passes must be presented to guards." That's all there is—the car, the building, the sign, and the sky. For me, at any rate, it has a charged talismanic significance.

19. THE POWER
OF WORDS

*In my youthful way I wondered, "If only some
day a hundred years from now, a little street or
even an alley could be named after me."*

STANISLAW ULAM,
Adventures of a Mathematician (1976)

It is time that gives power to words. There is no street
named after Ulam, but the day may still come. Ulam, a
Polish mathematician who came to the United States
shortly before World War II, has spent most of his life at
Los Alamos. There, in the early 1950s, he hit upon a clever
way to create the temperatures—hotter than the surface
of the sun—necessary for thermonuclear explosions. Oppenheimer once referred to Ulam's idea as "technically
sweet." The phrase seemed innocent enough at the time.
The consequences of Ulam's idea are certainly on a scale
to justify naming a street after him, perhaps a whole plaza.

People have already been talking about nuclear weapons for many decades. As early as 1921 the Austrian
nuclear physicist Hans Thirring, brooding on the implications of Einstein's theories, wondered what "might
happen in a town, if the dormant energy of a single brick
were to be let free, say in the form of an explosion." Now
we know. In the same decade Winston Churchill, possi-

bly spurred by H. G. Wells, speculated about future wars using intercontinental missiles with warheads of tremendous force. Fifty years later, when the great powers have thousands of such weapons, Churchill's idle wondering has taken on a prophetic cast. "Now we are in for trouble," said Oppenheimer back in the spring of 1945, after he had been appointed to the Interim Committee set up to advise Truman about the bomb. Think of the resonance which time has given to that word "trouble."

> *Why didn't I believe in the success of your work? If we had had this weapon in 1939, we would never have had this war. Now and in the future, Europe and the world are too small for a war. With such weapons available war will become unbearable for the human race.*
>
> ADOLF HITLER to WALTER DORNBERGER,
> chief of the German V-2 rocket
> program in July 1943

Time will tell us the meaning of Hitler's words. He probably intended to say that the potential scale of war in the future would prevent it from taking place. We all hope this will prove to be the case. But perhaps the real meaning is that we won't be able to "bear" such a war when it comes. Then again, we might "bear" it—more or less —and Hitler's remark will take on a tinge of irony. It's too soon to tell. In one sense his remark is already ironic. He died without knowing about the bomb.

There has been no shortage of warnings about that. It will take gall to plead ignorance when the time comes. Even before Hiroshima the men who made the bomb were beginning to have second thoughts, especially at the Met Lab in Chicago. But the mood of war was too strong.

Pity found no place in the hearts of the men managing the war. We had been the victims of atrocities and did not shrink from inflicting them on our enemies. Thousand-plane raids had destroyed whole cities. Now one plane could do the job. What was the difference?

We soon learned. I once hit a kid in school. It was a slap, really, but it landed solidly and hard. All the anger drained out through my arm and hand. I remember the sensation vividly. It left me at peace within. Nagasaki seems to have had some such effect in Washington. Japan had not yet surrendered but Truman issued orders that no more bombs were to be dropped. The nuclear core for a fourth was being assembled at that very moment in Los Alamos. In the bomb-making community Nagasaki dissipated the mood of war overnight. Hiroshima could pass muster as a military act, but Nagasaki seemed gratuitous, vindictive, and vengeful. Warnings began to pour forth from the alarmed scientists. "The bomb changed everything," said Einstein, "except our modes of thinking."

> *Mr. Byrnes's . . . view [was] that our possessing and demonstrating the bomb would make Russia more manageable in Europe.*
>
> LEO SZILARD, the physicist, describing a meeting with JAMES BYRNES in May 1945

Mr. Byrnes was wrong. Of course nobody can guess right every time, but even allowing for normal human error, the postwar military and political leaders of the United States seem to have got things wrong with uncanny persistence. The bomb, conceived as a weapon pure and simple so long as it belonged to us alone, had no apparent effect on Stalin at all. He seemed to dismiss it out of hand. The Americans found this disconcerting. After the first

Russian bomb was detonated in August, 1949, the United States embarked on a crash program to build the H-bomb. It was then that Stanislaw Ulam earned his right to a street. But the Russians were right behind us, and it has been that way ever since. The arms race has been a continually escalating spiral for nearly forty years, but neither side has gained a useful political advantage, much less one on a scale proportionate to the growing risk. Our relations with the Soviet Union now are pretty much what they were in the early 1950s, with the sole exception that now we have thousands of nuclear weapons with which to threaten them, instead of hundreds.

The curious thing is that this came as no surprise to the alarmed atomic scientists of the late 1940s. Even before the end of the war a group at the Chicago Met Lab warned there would be such an arms race in the absence of international agreement. One result of their warnings was the Acheson-Lilienthal plan of 1946, presented to the UN— after certain modifications—by Bernard Baruch on June 14th of that year. He opened by saying, "We are here to make a choice between the quick and the dead. . . . Let us not deceive ourselves: we must elect world peace, or world destruction." The plan probably had small chance of success even in its original form; Baruch's modifications settled the matter. The Russians rejected it. The arms race so often predicted duly followed.

Postwar history might be described as a contest of competing predictions. One group said nuclear weapons were too dangerous for the old international structure which accepted war as a last resort. They predicted disaster if we continued on our present course. A second group promised security through arms. In a letter to Eisenhower on February 6, 1956, Baruch said, "Whether we can get the 1500-mile [rocket] or the 5000-mile first, I do not know, but we should try for both. Whoever gets either one first will have the world by the tail with a downpull." That is a flat prediction. As it happened we got both first, but we did not get the world by the tail. Baruch's words sound hollow now.

It has to be asked why one group of predictions—for the most part accurate—has been ignored, while the failure of another group seems to have had so little effect. It is a curious business. One answer is that while the pessimists foresaw many things which have come to pass, their worst fears are not among them. We have had no big war. In the late 1940s the pessimists appeared to see everything in one blinding flash—a world armed to the teeth with nuclear weapons atop mighty missiles, engaged in a kind of push-button Buck Rogers war. They warned that others would soon build bombs, there would be no defense, America would have to disperse her cities, in the end war would come.

In 1945 the science fiction writer Robert Heinlein urged Americans to school themselves in woodcraft, so they might take to the wilderness in the event of nuclear war. His vision of the post-attack world was grim in the extreme: total collapse of communications, transportation, medical services, industry, the capacity of the government to govern. It reads a good deal like a study done in 1975 by the Congressional Office of Technology Assessment. Heinlein had got it about right, but he was premature. So it was with other pessimists. The level of arms they foresaw took years to come to pass. We have not even quite reached the Buck Rogers stage yet, but it is no longer far off. It used to take hours to retarget a Minuteman missile, for example. Now it can be done by punching numbers into a computer. If the MX system is ever built the missiles will be able to retarget themselves. They will conduct a kind of perpetual electronic conversation, keeping up with their fellows. If some are destroyed, the rest will reallocate the most important targets. But this may not arrive until 1990, nearly half a century after the pessimists first saw it coming.

And of course there has been no war. The traditionalists claim it is fear which has done the trick. The Soviets know what war will mean, they say, and it has made them sober and cautious. Without nuclear weapons we would have gone to war over Berlin in 1948, or over Cuba in 1962. Maybe so, and maybe not. My own view is that war is not something we launch deliberately, but something which happens to us. We move toward it at a glacial pace, responding to events. Accident, or fate, chooses the precise circumstances of the opening shot. Preparation for war determines the sort of war it will be. Nations fight with the weapons they *have*. But that is my view, and it is only an opinion. Others have their opinions. Only events can establish, after the fact, which was closest to the truth.

There is also another reason the pessimists have had so little effect on anything except our nightmares. Everyone —just about everyone—concedes that nuclear weapons are too dangerous for routine military use. But what are we to do about it? International agreements to limit arms seem to offer the only way out, so we have been trying to negotiate limits. It is a slow process. There is not much to show for it. We must keep on trying. But what do we do in the interim? From the point of view of both Moscow and Washington, "the other side" is building more weapons. "We" can't afford to fall behind. The pessimists may predict disaster in the future, but we have got to decide what to ask for in the defense budget today. So go on building weapons today, and make plans to negotiate limits tomorrow, and allow ourselves to hope, encour-

aged by years of peace of a kind, that things will go on
no worse than they have.

> *If atomic bombs are to be added as new weapons
> to the arsenals of a warring world, or to the
> arsenals of nations preparing for war, then the
> time will come when mankind will curse the
> names of Los Alamos and Hiroshima.*

> OPPENHEIMER in a speech accepting an award
> at Los Alamos on October 16, 1945

That is a flat prediction. The time of which Oppenheimer
spoke has not yet come. Last year I read an interesting
book by Horace Freeland Judson called *The Search for
Solutions*. It is an imaginative investigation of the scientific method. In it Judson writes that the best confirma-
tion of a scientific theory is a "strong prediction" which
is borne out by observation. In his theory of relativity, for
example, Einstein predicted that the gravitational effect of
stars would bend light rays. Experiment showed it was so.
This "strong prediction"—a flat, confident statement that
something would happen, based on a theory—convinced
the doubters of relativity.

It will be the same with the predictions of Oppenheimer and so many others. Their theory is a simple one.
It is that preparation for war leads to war. If nations are
ready for war and constantly push and test each other,
eventually things will slip out of their control and war
will follow. This view of war as a characteristic and habitual form of human behavior directly contradicts the more
hopeful view of the national security establishment.
There war is seen as something which needlessly follows
when the soldiers and statesmen haven't done their job
right. It is a bit as if members of a basketball team insisted

they could keep the ball in the air forever, if they were only serious enough about the effort, kept in training, and regularly rotated players. Common sense says someone would eventually drop the ball. The national security establishment insists it will never drop the ball, so long as we provide it with money, men, and arms, don't over-reach, and soberly warn our opponents of the conse-quences if they push too hard.

The warnings issued by the pessimists have been fre-quent, cogent, eloquent and persuasive—so it seems to me—but they have had little effect on anything except the rhetoric of national leaders. Everyone pays lip service to arms control and "peace," but that is as far as it goes. The pessimists' words elicit fear, but are too weak to achieve that final degree of conviction which might make them the basis of action. The problem seems to be that they still constitute no more than a theory, and others have other theories. Words are only words, after all. We should not expect words to achieve what Hiroshima could not. As time goes by without further use of nuclear weapons, the national security community seems to be confirmed in its theory, summed up by the Roman military writer Vegetius, who said, "If you want peace, prepare for war." Every passing year strengthens their belief that nuclear weapons make us safe. Indeed, the traditionalists think the argument has already been settled.

Of course the Romans had wars in plenty in spite of their preparations, but this is only a debater's point and it lacks the power to convince. No argument, by itself, can do that on a matter of such large, general importance. But somebody in this debate is wrong, and eventually we're going to know who it is. Perhaps we should see the postwar world as a kind of laboratory, engaged in a major experiment to test the theories of the pessimists and those who trust in arms. Both have made strong predictions. Eventually one or the other will be in a position to say they told us so. In this light the pessimists may properly see themselves as arguing before two audiences simultaneously—their contemporaries, whom they hope to warn in time; and the postwar survivors of the future, who will be in a position to test prewar theories against reality.

> . . . *the most ominous thing about these wars is that they were not isolated or unprecedented calamities. They were two wars in a series; and when we envisage the whole series in a synoptic view, we discover that this is not only a series but a progression. In our recent Western history war has been following war in an ascending order of intensity; and today it is already apparent that the war of 1939–45 was not the climax of this crescendo movement.*
>
> ARNOLD TOYNBEE,
> *War and Civilization* (1950)

In ancient times the gift of prophecy was held in something close to religious awe. It's not hard to see why. Events rarely spring out of nowhere. Once things have happened, their origins are usually clear. Thus the future is always hidden in the present, and yet it eludes us. Economists, stock analysts, and the Central Intelligence Agency all forecast the future in language as obscure as the pronouncements of the Delphic Oracle. This is not coyness, but a healthy instinct for professional self-preservation. Getting things generally right is a major achievement. Getting them *exactly* right is close to miraculous, and it doesn't often happen. Even science, which bases its predictions on an understanding of the structure of things, has about it an awesome quality inspiring trust. Thus the pessimists' warnings, merely persuasive as argument now, will acquire a new authority when borne out by events.

What the pessimists say is that nuclear weapons do not preclude a big war, and that when a big war comes nuclear weapons will be used in it. But that is as far as they go. What sort of war, when, how it will start, who will fight it—these things are all hidden from them. The question of nuclear war is sometimes posed in very stark terms, as if there were only two possibilities: the sort of armed peace we have had since 1945, or Armageddon—a cataclysm involving thousands of warheads, leaving the Northern Hemisphere a kind of smoking ruin, with a pitiful remnant of ragged survivors left to sift the debris. Things might turn out that way—there are weapons enough, certainly—but they might not.

War may come again not once but many times. Nuclear weapons may be used in Europe, or in the Middle East, or between Pakistan and India. They may wreck the world, or only a part of it, or only a city or two. Of one thing we can be sure: When it comes, the traditionalists will express deep surprise. But those who argue the matter afterwards will still tend to divide along the old lines. One group will say that these weapons threaten, not protect us. If we have them, we will eventually use them. *Look at what happened!* Their opponents will insist the case was a special one, that a change in strategy here, the rewording of a diplomatic note there, might have made all the difference. The evidence is certain to be fragmentary. The senselessness of the episode will make it seem like a kind of accident. The horror of it will encourage people to think it can never happen again, just as they did in 1945.

The argument will not be settled dramatically and all at once. But if the pessimists can state their case clearly enough in advance—refining the terms of the experiment, if you will—then gradually events will confirm the authority of what they say.

The essays collected in this book were all originally published in *Commonweal* magazine, sometimes under differ
ent titles from those used here. The dates of publication
follow:

1. Peace of a Sort	*June 4, 1976*
2. The Next War	*March 30, 1979*
3. On Disbelief	*January 15, 1982*
4. War by Computer	*December 7, 1979*
5. Signs of War	*February 27, 1981*
6. Spasm War	*March 27, 1981*
7. After the Bombs	*January 30, 1981*
8. What to Tell the Kids	*November 6, 1981*
9. Down the Miracle Mile	*April 24, 1981*
10. How Accurate Is Accurate?	*December 4, 1981*
11. Crossing the Nuclear Threshold	*October 10, 1980*
12. What Is War?	*April 9, 1982*
13. Back to the Cold War	*February 4, 1977*
14. A Question of Intentions	*December 19, 1980*
15. The Moral Fallacy	*September 11, 1981*
16. The Principles of Abolition	*July 31, 1981*
17. The Way Out Is Forward	*October 9, 1981*
18. Artifacts of the Recent Past	*June 19, 1981*
19. The Power of Words	*February 12, 1982*

Thomas Powers was on the staff of United Press International when he won a Pulitzer Prize in 1971 for his reporting on the case of the young Weatherman terrorist Diana Oughton. This work became the basis of his first book, *Diana: The Making of a Terrorist*. Since then he has published *The War at Home* (1973) and *The Man Who Kept the Secrets: Richard Helms and the CIA* (1979). Powers lives in New York City with his wife and three daughters.

A NOTE ON THE TYPE

This book was set via computer-driven cathrode-ray tube in Janson, a redrawing of type cast from matrices long thought to have been made by the Dutchman Anton Janson, who was a practicing type founder in Leipzig during the years 1668-87.However, it has been conclusively demonstrated that these types are actually the work of Nicholas Kis (1650-1702), a Hungarian, who most probably learned his trade from the master Dutch type founder Dirk Voskens. The type is an excellent example of the influential and sturdy Dutch types that prevailed in England up to the time William Caslon developed his own incomparable designs from them.

Composed, printed and bound by
The Haddon Craftsmen, Inc., Scranton, Pennsylvania

Typography and binding design
by Dorothy Schmiderer